John Gould taught at Christ Church, Oxford and University College, Swansea before becoming H.O.Wills Professor of Greek at the Univerity of Bristol. He is the author of *The Development of Plato's Ethics* (1955) and of a series of articles on Greek poetry and drama and on Greek religious and social institutions.

New thinking, rather than new data, distinguishes John Gould's lucid examination of Herodotus as historian; he brings new approaches to Herodotus' sources and to his methods of collecting information, to the logic of his narrative and to his understanding of human behaviour. Professor Gould draws on recent advances in the understanding of oral tradition, and takes issue with a number of current theories about the nature of Herodotus' historical thinking. Herodotus as storyteller, he argues, does not preclude Herodotus as historian; Herodotus' declared subject, the war between Persians and Greeks, is itself Herodotus' own construct, embodied in the form of continuous narrative which derives from a mass of local and family traditions that reach back more than a century into the past and extend to take in most of the known world. The idea of reciprocity is shown by Professor Gould to be the guiding principle of Herodotus' enquiry; it provides a logical rationale which stretches backwards and forwards through time and place, and forms the impetus which generates Herodotean narrative. It is, he decides, only a radical rejection of modern historiographical values that will bring us to the realization of Herodotus' historiographical importance: we must see him as enacting in narrative the social memory of his own generation.

In the same series

Roy Porter on *Gibbon*
Hugh Tulloch on *Acton*
Owen Dudley Edwards on *Macaulay*
Linda Colley on *Namier*
Nicholas Phillipson on *Hume*

forthcoming titles

David Cannadine on *Trevelyan*
Douglas Johnson on *Michelet*

Herodotus

John Gould

Herodotus

St. Martin's Press
New York

© John Gould 1989

First published in the United States of America in 1989

Printed in Great Britain

ISBN 0-312-02855-5

Library of Congress Cataloging-in-Publication Data

Gould, John, 1927—
    Herodotus/John Gould.
        p.   cm.—(Historians on historians)
    ISBN 0-312-02855-5
    1. Herodotus.   2. History, Ancient—Historiography.   I. Title.
II. Series.
D56.52.H45068   1989   89-10645
930'.072—dc20   CIP

Contents

Preface

When I was asked to contribute a short book on Herodotus to the present series, I accepted the invitation with alacrity and some misgiving. The book that follows has its roots in lectures delivered at Bristol over the past several years. Like the lectures, the book has as its central concern the mind of the historian; it tries to answer such questions as how he understands, assesses and makes use of the sources of information available to him; how he creates and structures a continuous narrative on the basis of these sources; how he makes sense of and explains to the reader the events of the historical past; and how he perceives, by means of notions of reciprocity and inversion, the alien world of other cultures and distant lands into which his historical enquiries have taken him. It does not, except very incidentally, address the question of Herodotus' reliability as a source for the history of the years covered by his narrative – and that, of course, is a question of central interest to most ancient historians of our own day. The omission exists for the good reason that I am not qualified to give an answer to the question, but it results in a book which some may feel avoids an issue crucial for any reading of Herodotus.

Writing the book has given me great pleasure, some of which, I hope, may reach the reader. The bulk of it was written while my family and I were guests of Greek friends: from their generosity, hospitality and open-minded curiosity about every aspect of the world I learned more (and more about Herodotus) than I can convey in the formal surroundings of a preface.

Earlier versions of chapter 4 ('Why Things Happen') have been given as a paper in Oxford, Bristol, Durham, Yale and the Center for Hellenic Studies, Washington, DC, and the final version has benefited greatly from discussion on all these

PREFACE

occasions. Many friends and colleagues have helped me,
sometimes unwittingly, with advice, argument and off-prints:
they include George Forrest, David Lewis, Alan Lloyd, James
Redfield, Geoffrey de Ste Croix, Michael Vickers and Thomas
Wiedemann. But above all the book is owed to my wife Gill
and daughter Tabitha: they have taken part in its writing
throughout and at every stage the book has been improved
by their critical responses. When, because of temporary problems with my sight, I was unable to correct the edited type-
script, my wife read over the whole to me and acted once
more as arbiter on point after point of lucidity and style,
so that the whole process of revision was one shared between
us. It has never been more true to say that without her the
book would never have been completed.

The translations throughout are my own (save for quotations from the Bible, where I have used the King James
version). I have translated the quotations from Herodotus
myself, rather than use the lucid and immensely readable
translation by Aubrey de Selincourt, published in the Penguin
Classics series, because I wanted to keep closer to the feel
and shape of Herodotus' Greek than de Selincourt's freer rein
allowed him to be.

J.G.
Bristol, Athens, Chania
February 1985 to March 1988

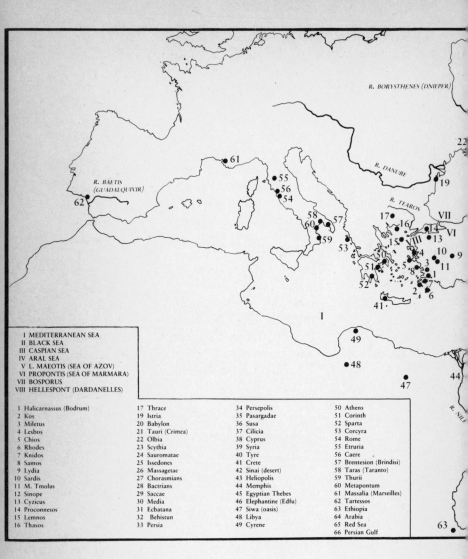

R. BORYSTHENES (DNIEPER)

R. BAETIS
(GUADALQUIVIR)

R. DANUBE

R. TEAROS

R. NILE

I MEDITERRANEAN SEA
II BLACK SEA
III CASPIAN SEA
IV ARAL SEA
V L. MAEOTIS (SEA OF AZOV)
VI PROPONTIS (SEA OF MARMARA)
VII BOSPORUS
VIII HELLESPONT (DARDANELLES)

1 Halicarnassus (Bodrum)
2 Kos
3 Miletus
4 Lesbos
5 Chios
6 Rhodes
7 Knidos
8 Samos
9 Lydia
10 Sardis
11 M. Tmolus
12 Sinope
13 Cyzicus
14 Proconnesos
15 Lemnos
16 Thasos

17 Thrace
19 Istria
20 Babylon
21 Tauri (Crimea)
22 Olbia
23 Scythia
24 Sauromatae
25 Issedones
26 Massagetae
27 Chorasmians
28 Bactrians
29 Saccae
30 Media
31 Ecbatana
32 Behistun
33 Persia

34 Persepolis
35 Pasargadae
36 Susa
37 Cilicia
38 Cyprus
39 Syria
40 Tyre
41 Crete
42 Sinai (desert)
43 Heliopolis
44 Memphis
45 Egyptian Thebes
46 Elephantine (Edfu)
47 Siwa (oasis)
48 Libya
49 Cyrene

50 Athens
51 Corinth
52 Sparta
53 Corcyra
54 Rome
55 Etruria
56 Caere
57 Brentesion (Brindisi)
58 Taras (Taranto)
59 Thurii
60 Metapontum
61 Massalia (Marseilles)
62 Tartessos
63 Ethiopia
64 Arabia
65 Red Sea
66 Persian Gulf

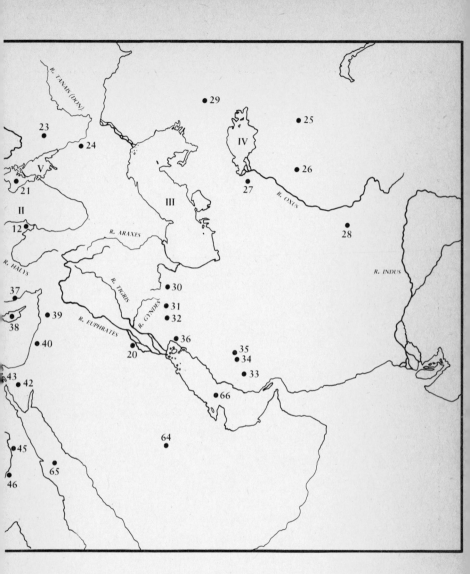

R. TANAIS (DON)

23

24

V

21

II

12

R. HALYS

37

38

39

40

43

42

45

46

65

64

III

R. ARAXES

R. TIGRIS

R. GYNDES

R. EUPHRATES

20

36

30

31

32

66

29

IV

27

25

26

R. OXUS

28

R. INDUS

35

34

33

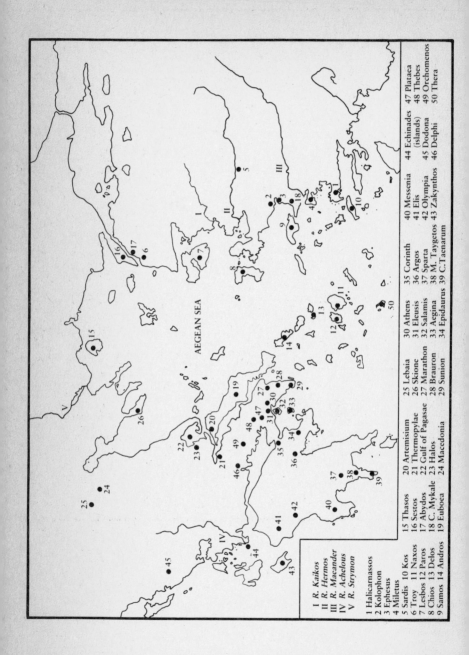

AEGEAN SEA

I R. Kaikos
II R. Hermos
III R. Macander
IV R. Achelous
V R. Strymon

1 Halicarnassos
2 Kolophon
3 Ephesus
4 Miletus
5 Sardis   10 Kos
6 Troy   11 Naxos
7 Lesbos   12 Paros
8 Chios   13 Delos
9 Samos   14 Andros

15 Thasos
16 Sestos
17 Abydos
18 C. Mykale
19 Euboea

20 Artemisium   25 Lebaia
21 Thermopylae   26 Skione
22 Gulf of Pagasae 27 Marathon
23 Halos   28 Brauron
24 Macedonia   29 Sunion

30 Athens
31 Eleusis
32 Salamis
33 Aegina
34 Epidaurus

35 Corinth   40 Messenia   44 Echinades
36 Argos   41 Elis   (islands)
37 Sparta   42 Olympia   45 Dodona
38 M. Taygetos   43 Zakynthos   46 Delphi
39 C.Taenarum

47 Plataea
48 Thebes
49 Orchomenos
50 Thera

Introduction

In the middle of the fifth century BC, a Greek called Herodotus wrote a narrative of the conflict between Greeks and the Persian empire which had come to a climax, little more than a generation earlier, in the battles of Thermopylae, Salamis and Plataea (480–79 BC). He called his narrative an 'enquiry' (the Greek word is *historie*) and thus brought the word 'history' in its modern sense into the vocabulary of Europe and the West. Herodotus had come to believe that the great Persian invasion of the Greek mainland in 480 had its origins, not just in the failure of an earlier punitive expedition which had been defeated ten years earlier at Marathon, but more remotely in everything that had flowed from the absorption into the Persian empire of the kingdom of Lydia (in what is now north-western Turkey) more than half a century before. He therefore began his narrative with the fall of the Lydian kingdom under its last king, Croesus, and the events that led up to it, and continued from that point with Persian expansion into other parts of the eastern Mediterranean littoral and the shores of the Black Sea under four Persian kings: Cyrus the Great, Cambyses, Dareius and finally Xerxes, who led the invasion of 480.

He saw his narrative, in his own words, as the record of 'astonishing and heroic achievements', but the whole tenor of his writing carries the implication that he saw it also as a story of conflict between alien cultures: the narrative includes description not only of Persian culture but also of the cultures of Egypt and the Scythian tribes, and on a smaller scale of the many other tribes and peoples in Africa, Asia and south-eastern Europe who came into contact with the expanding power of Persia. Though he writes as a Greek and though his narrative unsurprisingly takes Greek culture as definitive of what is 'normal' in human experience, Herodotus' account of other cultures is not an account simply of barbarous, primitive and uncivilized behaviour. Herodotus is an astonishingly unprejudiced observer of humanity in its variety.

At some point after his death, probably in the altogether different world that followed the death of Alexander the Great in 323 BC, Herodotus' narrative was divided into nine 'books', and these in turn into sections and subsections (hence references to his text take the form of citing book, section and subsection, e.g. 3.125.2). The first book deals with the fall of Lydia, the rise of Persia under Cyrus the Great and the consolidation of Persian power in Asia Minor, up to the death of Cyrus in 530 BC. Book Two is taken up with a huge excursus on the geography, culture and history of Egypt, which was to be the target of the next phase of Persian expansion, under Cyrus' son Cambyses. Book Three continues the story to cover the death of Cambyses in July or August 522 BC, the period of crisis and unrest in Persia which followed, the eventual emergence of Dareius as the new king and the establishment of his power. Book Four deals with Dareius' attempt to conquer the Scythian tribes who lived north and east of the Danube and in southern Russia, and with Persian expansion into north Africa. Book Five opens with the Persian conquest of the north coast of the Aegean and the Thracian tribes of what is today northern Greece and the southern Balkans. It continues with the abortive attempt by the Greek cities of the Turkish coast to break free of Persian control (the so-called 'Ionian revolt'), and with the intervention of Athens in that revolt. Book Six begins the story of Persian attempts to avenge what they saw as Greek interference in the affairs of the Persian empire, and the first seaborne expedition against European Greece which was defeated at Marathon in 490 BC. The last three books cover the great invasion of the Greek mainland of 480–79 undertaken by Dareius' son, Xerxes; the story ends with the fight against Persia being carried back across the Aegean to the coast of Turkey itself.

Because Herodotus' narrative is the first example of 'historical' narrative in the European tradition (he was early on given the somewhat ambivalent title of 'father of history'), the way in which he defines his subject-matter contains surprises for the modern reader brought up in a different tradition of historical writing, one which goes back to Herodotus but of which he is not a part. The chapters which follow are concerned with that definition of 'history', with Herodotus' sources and methods of enquiry, and with his perception of human experience and of the 'world' described by his narrative.

1 The World of Herodotus

The king of kings, Dareius son of Hystaspes, to his slave Gadatas speaks as follows: I learn that you are not in all things obeying my commands. In that you work my land, planting fruit trees from beyond the Euphrates in the regions of lower Asia, I commend your purpose and because of it there shall be stored up for you great gratitude in the king's house. But in that you destroy my ordering of things on the gods' behalf, I will give you experience, unless you change your ways, of outraged feeling: you have been levying payments from the sacred gardeners of Apollo and have commanded them to till land that is not sacred, disregarding the mind of my ancestors towards the god who spoke the whole truth to the Persians and . . .[1]

This tantalizing fragment is the king of Persia, the Great King as the Greeks called him, writing, perhaps a generation before the birth of Herodotus, to one of the two dozen or so most powerful men in the Persian empire, the satrap (governor) of the Ionian province on the west coast of Turkey. The language of the original inscription is Greek, but it seems perfectly to catch the tone of voice and to reflect the attitudes of the Persian king in his dealings with his great officials: it was a tone with which Herodotus shows some familiarity.[2] The satrap is addressed as the king's 'slave': so, too, Dareius in his account of his own achievements in the inscription at Behistun refers to others of his greatest officials as his 'bondsmen';[3] the concern with cultivation and the planting of trees is attested for other Persian kings and reflected in our word 'paradise' from the Median word for 'garden'. Both his way of addressing the satrap and his passion for trees are things that would have surprised, and in the first case affronted, most Greeks, as would also Dareius' concern for the rights and privileges of priests. (This last is a concern which seems likely to be based on a misapprehension of the political power of priests in Greek communities: it has been plausibly suggested that Dareius was influenced by the power wielded by priests in Egyptian society, where he seems also to have been at pains to reinstate threatened priestly privileges and immunities.[4] If so, we have an interesting sidelight on Persian misunderstanding of Greek culture.) But Herodotus is not 'most Greeks' and his judgments are his own. A look at his background will help to show us why.

His sensitivity to the customs of an alien culture and to the ways of an autocratic ruler is not just the product of his own qualities of mind and personality: it is also a part of Herodotus' inheritance from the world into which he was born. Herodotus belonged to the people whom the Persians called Yauna and whom we call Ionian Greeks. Halicarnassus (now Bodrum), the town where he was born, lies on the Turkish coast just north of the island of Kos, at the extreme western edge of the vast empire over which the Persian kings ruled from their capital at Susa, three months journey away in western Iran, near the head of the Persian Gulf.[5] In spite of its location inside the Persian empire, Halicarnassus was a Greek city: its language, religion, coinage, institutions, culture and politics were all Greek. For Herodotus, we must realize, to be Greek was not a matter of geography; it was not to live in what we call Greece, but rather, to quote his own definition of 'Greekness', in a famous passage, it was 'being of the same blood and tongue, having in common temples of the gods and sacrifices, and shared customs' (8.144.2), and by that definition there is no question of his Greekness, or of his city's.

But Halicarnassus was nonetheless a city on the margin between two cultures: it was a harbour town on its own peninsula. Inland lay the territory of the Carians (to the Persians, Karka) who, with the Greeks of the coastal towns, had been absorbed into the Persian empire along with the kingdom of Lydia when that kingdom fell to Cyrus the Great in about 545 BC. The arrival of 'the Mede' (that is, Cyrus' Median general, Harpagus) on the Aegean coast had been a traumatic event, remembered with pain long afterwards as a watershed in history; 'How old were you when the Mede came?' is a haunting line in a fragmentary poem by Xenophanes, who came from Colophon, to the north of Halicarnassus, lived through the event as a young man and recalled it in a poem written in his nineties.[6] In 499 BC the Carians joined with the Greeks of the coastal towns in revolting from Persian control. Like the other towns of the coast to the north and south, Halicarnassus had been founded by Greek settlers five hundred years before Herodotus was born, but intermarriage with the Carians of the interior had evidently been common, so that Greek and Carian stock were well mixed by Herodotus' day. It has been calculated that almost half of the more than 250 known names of citizens of Halicarnassus in the fifth century BC are Carian. In many cases Greek and Carian names are borne indifferently in successive generations of the same family; not only did men of clear Carian descent give their sons Greek names but, perhaps more surprisingly, the opposite also occurs in a significant number of cases.[7] It is clear that we are not dealing with a town in which Hellenized Carians are trying to become absorbed into a new culture and to lose all traces of their non-Greek origins; on the contrary, it seems that Halicarnassians of Carian descent retained their pride in their family origins and that in some sense at least there is parity of status between Greek and non-Greek. Mixture of race and culture was a common occurrence in the Persian empire, which combined an astonishing degree of detailed interference in distant local communities with an equally astonishing level of tolerance for religious and cultural variety: it has recently been pointed out that Elephantine (Edfu in Upper Egypt), a town with a Greek name, garrisoned by Jews commanded by an Iranian, had as one of its inhabitants a Chorasmian from Afghanistan north of the Oxus. The Persian king himself, in a letter to the garrison commander in 419 BC, lays down the days of unleavened bread and orders abstinence from beer-drinking and respite from work.[8]

One of the best-known and longest fifth-century inscriptions from Halicarnassus mentions a number of Halicarnas-

sians by name: several (such as Leon, Phormio and Appollo-
nides) have unambiguously Greek names but Carian fathers;
one (Megabates) has a name that should be Persian, with
a father (Aphyasis) who looks to be Carian. One of the Carian
names, that of the father of Phormio, is Panyassis: the name
is also that of a Halicarnassian epic poet, a considerable figure
in the history of Greek epic, who is said by our sources to
have been Herodotus' cousin or uncle and to have been
involved with him in the political struggles at Halicarnassus
which led eventually to Herodotus' departure into lifelong
exile and to Panyassis' death.[9] Herodotus' own family, though
it is said to have been one of the 'noble' families of Halicarnassus (and there is no reason to doubt the assertion), seems
to show the same mixture of Greek and Carian names that
we find elsewhere in the city. So we ought to be the less surprised that in the very first sentence of his *History* Herodotus
sets the achievements of Greeks and non-Greeks, and by implication their interest to his audience, on a level, side by side,
and promises to record both for posterity and to ensure their
lasting renown.

But Halicarnassus was not merely open to influences from
the non-Greek East by virtue of its geographical position.
It was also, as Herodotus' own work shows, part of the
thought-world that had been created already in the sixth century BC by the philosophical and scientific thinkers who
worked in Miletus, some forty miles or so to the north of
Halicarnassus, and in other Ionian Greek cities. Here too
Halicarnassus is very much a town between two worlds. The
Greeks who around 1000 BC colonized the Aegean coast of
Turkey and the offshore islands, and their descendants in
the fifth century, thought of themselves as belonging to three
distinct and mutually competing segments of the Greek
people: in the north, including the island of Lesbos, Aeolians;
in the centre, from Chios and the Kaikos and Hermos valleys
south to Halicarnassus, Ionians; and in the south, from Kos
to Rhodes with the mainland town of Knidos opposite, Dor-
ians. Halicarnassus claimed to have been founded by Greeks
from Troizen in the eastern Peloponnese – that is, by Greeks
on the fringes of the Dorian area of mainland Greece – and

had once, so Herodotus (1.144) reports, been a member of a Dorian league of six cities. It had been expelled from the league at some unspecified date, because of the actions of a Halicarnassian called Agasikles, who had broken the religious customs of a common athletic and religious festival of the Dorian Greeks in honour of Triopean Apollo. Whatever the truth of that tradition (which looks like a claim to ultimate marginality), and despite Herodotus' own often disparaging remarks about the Ionians, it is clear both from literary evidence and from documents that in the fifth century Halicarnassus was purely Ionic in language and culture, and Herodotus himself writes a form of Greek that unmistakably associates him with the intellectual world of Miletus, Ephesus and Colophon to the north, and not with the much less intellectual Dorian Greeks south of Halicarnassus. Herodotus' own apparent perception of himself as a Greek without clear and exclusive ties to either of the rival segments of Greek colonists is itself interesting and says something of his relative cultural and intellectual freedom and lack of constraining loyalties. Nonetheless, it is an aspect of Herodotus' distinctively Ionian Greek connections that we encounter in his use of words like *historie* (enquiry) and *physis* (nature). The outstanding and specific achievement of the Ionians, and in the first place of three thinkers who worked in Miletus in the first half of the sixth century (Thales, Anaximander and Anaximenes), had been to bring about 'a general increase of awareness and the application of intelligence to things', as a recent writer has put it;[10] of that 'greater awareness' Herodotus is markedly representative. He knows something of the intellectual reputation of Thales, though he doubts some of the traditions that reached him about Thales (1.74-5; 170), and also of Pythagoras (4.95-6) who came from Samos, an island where Herodotus spent some years of political exile.

Herodotus' interest in the puzzling phenomenon of the Nile floods is a good example both of his intellectual curiosity and of his critical approach to attempted explanation; the problem, and some traces of the method of argument, also occur in our evidence for the activities of the Milesians and their successors.[11] The problem arises, of course, from the fact that, unlike any European or Near Eastern river of which Greeks had experience, the Nile flooded in high summer when 'normal' rivers were at their lowest levels: it was this fact that above all caused Egypt to be regarded by most Greeks as a land where the world was turned upside down and where magical, impossible things could be expected to happen. Herodotus is not without his own commitment to such ideas, as we shall see. But for the Nile floods he seeks an explanation as 'scientific' and unmysterious as any of his Ionian predecessors and contemporaries, and he discards at least one explanation (2.20.2–3) – that the river floods when it does because its passage through the delta to the sea is prevented by the etesian winds which commonly blow from the north in high summer – on grounds that have rightly been seen as fully representative of fifth-century Greek scientific thought.[12] He points out that the explanation is unsatisfactory because (a) the Nile floods even when the etesians are not blowing, and (b) the etesians do not cause the same phenomenon in other rivers in North Africa and the Middle East which 'face' them, in spite of the fact that the flow of these rivers is weaker than that of the Nile.

Herodotus, one might say, comes close to making the word *historie* his own: together with its associated verbs he uses it twenty-three times. He almost certainly did not invent it, though the evidence for its earlier use by others is tantalizingly thin and unhelpful. Heraclitus is said to have used it in a disparaging and characteristically double-edged remark about Pythagoras, and the adjective *histor* (knowledgeable, expert), also used by Heraclitus, is as old as Homer and Hesiod in the sense of a 'good judge' of some matter. But it is, significantly, above all the verb, denoting precisely the activity of questioning, enquiring, researching, that is most frequent in Herodotus, most often used of his own enquiries but also repeatedly of the characters in his narrative. Asking questions, especially about other cultures, is a characteristically Herodotean activity. Perhaps one should say particularly Herodotean, rather than simply Greek or even Ionian Greek: Arnaldo Momigliano has pointed out that whereas Herodotus, in the East, was able to discover much about the culture of inland tribes both from his own enquiries and from other Greeks, especially the colonists of the Black Sea coastal towns, the Greeks of Massalia (Marseilles) in the West represented a very different and much less open society concerned at all costs to preserve its purely Greek tradition, afraid of contamination from non-Greek neighbours and generally incurious about the culture of its own hinterland.[13] Nothing could be further from Herodotus' cast of mind; and to say, as Momigliano does, however truly, that 'ancient travellers did not find it easy to go into the interior of countries', and that Halicarnassus is a coastal town, is only part of the explanation for such ignorance: enquiry, given the necessary curiosity, might, as Momigliano also points out, range further than men could travel, as Herodotus' does.

At this point, we perhaps need to remind ourselves that the enquiry denoted by the word *historie* in Herodotus' day has no specific, still less exclusive, connection with 'history' in the modern sense: Pythagoras is said to have used it of mathematical researches, and in the generation after Herodotus Democritus, the author of the atomic theory of the composition of matter, used it both as the title of one of his writings and as a word to describe his own enquires into the nature of matter; the playwright Euripides uses *historie* to refer to intellectual enquiry of all kinds.[14] It is only as a result of Herodotus' own use of the word to describe his work that the meaning 'history' in our sense is established, and that fact itself may be helpful when we come to consider Herodotus' own perception of his role as researcher and writer. Distinctions between areas of intellectual activity or spheres of interest which have come to seem fundamental to the mapping of human rational enquiry did not exist for the Greek thinkers of the sixth and fifth centuries BC. A good example is to be found in a famous fragment of Heraclitus, in which he writes scornfully of the 'much learning' of four of his predecessors and contemporaries: 'much learning does not teach intelligence; if it did, it would have taught Hesiod and Pythagoras, or again Xenophanes and Hecataeus' (fr. B 40 Diels-Kranz). These four men we should class, respectively, as a poet who wrote on cosmogonic and didactic themes, a philo-

sopher and religious 'sage'; a religious and perhaps philosophical poet, and a geographer and collector of oral traditions;
but our distinctions are not of interest to Heraclitus, and in
all likelihood not to Herodotus either. Moreover, by using
the word *historie* Herodotus aligns himself, perhaps deliberately, with a tradition of positivist thinking and rational analysis of available data which had been created in Ionia over
the past century.[15]

'Enquiry' meant many things for Herodotus, among them
and above all perhaps travel and the active pursuit of data.
The Egyptian priests of Memphis told Herodotus that,
according to their tradition, the god Herakles had been worshipped at Memphis for more than seventeen thousand years
before Egypt became part of the Persian empire. This claim
astonished him, since it implied that Herakles had been acknowledged as a god in Egypt thousands of years before his
birth according to Greek tradition as son of Zeus, *a fortiori*
before any Greek community could claim to have worshipped
him. Herodotus goes on to tell us that, to find out whether
other non-Greeks had the same tradition as the Egyptians,
he travelled to the Phoenician city of Tyre (in southern Leba-
non), 'discovering that there was a particularly sacred holy
place of Herakles there too'. The Phoenician priests told him,
in answer to his questions, that their sanctuary was as old
as the city of Tyre itself – that is, 2300 years old. Herodotus
'noticed' another holy place of Herakles at Tyre, called the
holy place of Herakles the Thasian. He therefore travelled
to Thasos, in the northern Aegean off the coast of Thrace,
where he found a sanctuary of Herakles built by the Phoenician founders of Thasos in the course of their voyage in search
of Europa; that, Herodotus calculates, was at least five generations before any Greek date for the birth of Herakles. Herodotus therefore concludes, in defiance of Greek tradition –
which gave Herakles a double parentage, both divine and
human – that Herakles, son of Zeus, was a different person
from the mortal Herakles, son of Amphitryon. It was the
latter whose birthdate was recorded in Greek tradition, while
the Greeks owed their knowledge of the divine Herakles to
the Egyptians.[16] That particular, and one might think mar-

ginal, enquiry (2.43.4–44) involved Herodotus in travelling literally the length and breadth of the eastern Mediterranean, and led him to infer a clear and, as it appeared to him, well-founded distinction between two different supernatural powers both named Herakles, one a god of great antiquity, the other what the Greeks called a hero, a mortal human being whose more than human powers are still active from the grave and whose grave is therefore a place of pilgrimage, miracles and ritual observance.

Herodotus writes as a travelled man. Curiosity and, it seems likely, the company of traders and merchants took him into the far reaches of the world where Greeks mixed with and bordered on non-Greeks. He talks of enquiries made in southern Italy, round the shores of the Black Sea, at Dodona in north-west Greece, in Egypt, at Cyrene in Libya; of things seen on the Dnieper in southern Russia, in Babylon on the Euphrates; of talking to Carthaginians and to the inhabitants of Delphi. He compares a word used by the native Celtic tribesmen north of Marseilles with one he took to be the same heard in Cyprus (5.9.3); the grain harvests of the black soil of Kinyps in Libya with those of the country round Babylon (4.198.2); weasels to be seen in the silphium fields around Cyrene with those of Tartessos in Spain (4.192.3). Confronted with tales of a pitch lake on an island off the coast of North Africa that he had not seen, he is prepared to consider the story possible: he has seen for himself pitch drawn from a lake on the island of Zakynthos off the west coast of the Peloponnese (4.195.2–4). He describes as an eyewitness the circular rafts of skin stretched over a frame of osier which are floated down the Euphrates until they reach Babylon, where they are dismantled and carried back upstream on donkeys (1.194). Above all, it is the ease and range of his geographical references that proclaim the traveller who has a lifetime of memories to draw on. To convey to his audience the distance up river from the Nile delta to Heliopolis, he offers the journey from the altar of the Twelve Gods in the agora of Athens to the sanctuary of Zeus at Olympia (2.7.1–2): he had made the journey to Heliopolis, he says, to check whether the traditions told him by the priests there would tally with those he had heard already from the priests at Memphis (he then had travelled on upriver to Egyptian Thebes for the same purpose). To illustrate the strangeness of the Taurian communities in the Crimea, living on a peninsula with the whole of the hinterland stretching behind them populated by alien Scythian tribesmen, he offers two imaginary parallels: the southern tip of Attica round Sunium, were it populated by non-Athenians, or, for those of his audience who have not made the voyage round the coast of Attica, an Italian alternative – the heel of Italy from Brindisi to Taranto as it would be if it were settled by non-Iapygians (4.99.4–5). When he argues for the idea that the land of Lower Egypt has been produced over many centuries by the silting action of the Nile, he produces from his own experience two possible examples of the same process on a smaller scale: the north-eastern coastline of Turkey from Troy south to the Maeander valley, and the silting up of the mouth of the Achelous in north-west Greece which had already joined half the islands of the Echinades group to the mainland (2.10). Familiarity with traders and their life is everywhere apparent: a good example is another passing reference, this time in his account of the founding of Cyrene by men from Thera. A reconnoitring party stranded on an island off the coast of north Africa is rescued by a Samian ship sailing to Egypt, blown off course by adverse winds. Continuing easterly winds carry them all the way to Spain, to Tartessos: Tartessos, Herodotus explains, was then still unexploited as a trading centre, and the Samians made more profit on their cargo when they returned home from there than any whom Herodotus had certain knowledge of – 'except,' he adds, 'Sostratus, the son of Laodamas from Aegina' (4.152.1–3). This is Sostratus' only appearance in Herodotus and scholars have understandably inferred that he too made his money trading to Tartessos: we now know they were wrong. Sostratus traded to Etruria, where an altar dedicated by him at Caere, just north of Rome, has recently been found. He too, and his fame as a trader, were part of Herodotus' world.

We do not know what turned Herodotus the Halicarnassian into a traveller because he does not tell us, but the political struggles of his city and his part in them are as likely an explanation as any. The details, and the chronology, are obscure. They involved the attempt to oust the local 'tyrant', a hereditary power-holder who controlled the city with the backing of his Persian overlords. The attempt seems at first to have been successful, but soon afterwards something went wrong: Herodotus' cousin was killed and Herodotus himself crossed to the island of Samos and seems never to have returned. In the opening words of his work he calls himself a Halicarnassian, but to all intents and purposes he was stateless, and tradition recorded that he died and was buried at Thurii in southern Italy: indeed, some versions of his text made him refer to himself in those opening words as 'Herodotus the Thurian'. The version of the text that Aristotle read seems to have had that wording. But 'Herodotus the Halicarnassian' is almost certainly how he thought of himself during his long political exile.

At some point in that exile he must have talked long and often to Athenians, almost certainly in Athens itself. Certainly his work was known in Athens: in a play written in 425 BC, the Athenian comic playwright Aristophanes offers an account of the outbreak of the war then being fought between Athens and Sparta which is patently a parody of the opening chapters of Herodotus' work.[17] Moreover, Herodotus is soaked in the political gossip and slander of Athenian society to an extent that can hardly be accounted for except by assuming that he became familiar at least with the politically active families at Athens: the Alcmaeonidae, the family of Pericles on his mother's side, may have been among them. He knows, for example, of the malicious rumours about how the Athenian tyrant Peisistratus refused to consummate his marriage with the daughter of Pericles' maternal great-grandfather because the family had a curse upon it (1.61.1–2); he has a somewhat disparaging version of the political career of Themistocles which must come from hostile Athenian sources (7.143.1); he reports a private remark of the Persian king Artaxerxes, made at the Persian capital to envoys from Argos, for which the witness cited is the Athenian Hipponicus, son of Kallias. Hipponicus was allegedly the wealthiest Athenian of Herodotus' own generation and a man prominent in Athenian cultural and intellectual life, who happened himself to be in Susa on diplomatic business (7.151); and he talks of conversations at firsthand with other leading Athenian political figures.

Athens certainly left its mark on Herodotus. The influence of his Athenian experiences is most marked in his political comments. His account of the battle of Salamis has a version of the words and actions of the Corinthian naval commander, Adeimantus, and stories of Corinthian reluctance to fight, especially under Athenian command, which are (as Herodotus saw) clearly tendentious and which Herodotus attributes specifically to his Athenian sources: Corinth was never a very popular city in Athenian eyes, and particularly not in the years when Herodotus was probably gathering the material for his work. Elsewhere in his narrative he ends his version of the political reforms of Kleisthenes at the end of the sixth century BC, which he saw as laying the foundations of democracy at Athens or, as he also calls it, 'equality of speech' with an ecstatic and somewhat misleading account of how the new freedom from tyranny released reserves of power and confidence which enabled her to achieve successes that would have been unthinkable only a generation before (5.78). We seem to hear an echo of the political language of fifth-century Athens here, as we almost certainly do in another remarkable passage, the so-called Persian debate in Book Three (3.80–2). Here one of Dareius' closest associates, Otanes the son of Pharnaspes, and Dareius' fellow conspirator in the plot which put Dareius on the Persian throne, is made to deliver an impassioned speech against autocracy and in favour of rule by the majority, equality under the law and the power of the people. The language and arguments of Otanes' speech clearly derive from the language of Athenian political debate in Herodotus' own day and have numerous parallels in contemporary Athenian literature.

So strong and so pervasive is the flavour of Athenian cultural life in the text of Herodotus that it is often simply taken for granted that the audience for whom Herodotus composed his work was itself Athenian. Major inferences about his purposes in writing have been based on that assumption: the whole tenor of his account of the war between Persians and Greeks has been supposed to derive in a quite specific way from Herodotus' reading of the political, and in particular the international, situation of Athens in his own day, and to be addressed to that situation and to its implications for Athenians as he saw them.[18] In fact it is not altogether obvious for whom Herodotus is writing: I have already quoted a passage in which he gives a south Italian geographical example to illustrate a point that he is making for an audience unfamiliar with the coastline of Attica. When in the first book he comes to describe the political situation at Athens and at Sparta as it was a hundred years or more earlier in the sixth century, just before the fall of the Lydian kingdom to the Persian armies (1.56-8), it is not clear that he takes for granted any greater familiarity about the situation in Athens and about Athenian tradition than he does for Sparta; his proclaimed subject at the outset is Greek, not Athenian, achievements in the Persian wars. His judgments on Athens are not uniformly favourable: though he tells his audience firmly (7.139.1-5), with an acknowledgment that the assertion will not be welcome to most of them, that he believes the Athenian decision to abandon Athens and the countryside of Attica to the enemy and fight alongside the other Greeks at Salamis was crucial to the defeat of Persia, so that the whole of Greece was saved by Athens, in another place (5.97.2) he comments that the vote of the Athenian assembly to send twenty ships to support the Ionian Greeks in their attempt to break away from Persian control in 500 BC was not only the beginning of disaster for Greeks and non-Greeks alike but also a classic illustration of the proposition that it is easier to fool a mass audience than a single individual: the Spartan king had refused the same request for help, supported by the same arguments, that the Athenian assembly granted.

Later tradition had Herodotus first present his work in Athens and be rewarded for it by a vote of the assembly of 60,000 drachmas, a considerable fortune. But then later tradition recorded many things about Herodotus that are clearly untrue, such as that his anti-Corinthian stories are the result of *their* refusal to pay him. Only one thing is relatively clear about Herodotus' original audience: that it was an audience rather than a readership. The opening words of his work, crudely translated, run: 'What follows is a performance [literally, "display"] of the enquiries of Herodotus from Halicarnassus.' The word Herodotus uses (*apodexis*) is the same word he uses for the heroic actions 'displayed' by Greeks and non-Greeks in the war of which he is to write: both are put on show. We have almost certainly to imagine Herodotus reading aloud his text, in whole or part, to an audience gathered to hear him perform: to translate Herodotus' word as 'publication' is to accommodate what he takes for granted to our own assumptions about how a literary work reaches those for whom it is written. Herodotus is composing his huge narrative for a world in which the dissemination of literature is still essentially oral, as it still was for Thucydides in the next generation.[19]

One last point to end this first chapter. I have been consistently and deliberately vague about the chronology of Herodotus' life and writings. The traditional date for Herodotus' birth, 484 BC, though it may well not be far out, is very probably based on nothing more than two characteristic assumptions of ancient biographical chronology: the first that a man's prime (his *akme* in Greek) occurs when he is forty; the second that his *akme* will coincide with some notable public event of his lifetime – in Herodotus' case, probably the foundation of the city of Thurii where he is said to have lived his last years and died. Taken together these two assumptions give us his birthdate, and as a form of proof the method is clearly worthless. Documentary evidence for Herodotus' life will not have existed, and it is unlikely that anyone was concerned to record the facts until long after anyone who had known him was still alive. The best we can do is to make such inferences as we can from what Herodotus himself says and does not say. Though he frequently tells us of things he has seen and heard for himself, he nowhere claims to have witnessed any of the events of the years actually covered by his narrative, and more than once cites others by name as eyewitnesses of what he records. It is therefore almost certain that he was not there to witness those events, and highly probable that this is because he was too young to have done so. As to the date of his death, we have again to make plausible guesses. He mentions in passing several events which we can date for certain to the opening years of the so-called Peloponnesian War between Athens and Sparta, but to nothing that we know to have happened after the early 420s BC: it seems highly likely that Herodotus died soon after 430 BC. If so, he was probably still in his fifties. But there is no reason to think that he died with his work unfinished. His choice of an ending has surprised and disconcerted some modern readers, and the assumption that Herodotus meant to continue has provided a convenient explanation. But the sense of incongruity is more likely due to our lack of sensitivity to Herodotus' own criteria for determining the proper shape of a narrative, as I hope to show below.

2 'Enquiry' and 'Social Memory'

> Dowayo baffled me at first by the way in which they used their categories prescriptively. 'Who organised this festival?' I would ask.
>
> 'The man with the porcupine quills in his hair.'
>
> 'I can't see anyone with porcupine quills in his hair.'
>
> 'No, he's not wearing them.'
>
> Things were always described as they should be, not as they were.
>
> Nigel Barley, *The Innocent Anthropologist*[1]

The problems of communication of a British anthropologist confronted with a West African tribe may help to remind us that asking questions and getting answers is not always as simple a process as we might unthinkingly take it to be. Herodotus' enquiries will certainly have had their difficult moments, and in this chapter I want to consider some of the sources, methods and methodological problems that lie behind his finished work. Of course, sometimes the nature of the question asked and the answer received, because questioner and respondent share cultural assumptions, will have been straightforward enough. Herodotus has a story (9.16, especially 16.5) of the banquet which a Theban called Attaginos gave for the Persian commander, Mardonios, and fifty leading Persian notables together with fifty of the leading Greeks from the locality, some days before the battle of Plataea in the summer of 479 BC.[2] Herodotus' source for this story is named as one of the Greeks present, a leading aristocrat from Orchomenos by the name of Thersandros. Thersandros' story (which is reported throughout in indirect speech) included details of a conversation he himself had had with his Persian neighbour on the same couch at the banquet. The unnamed Persian spoke Greek (according to Thersandros)

19

and asked Thersandros where he came from, telling him, in tears, so that Thersandros might preserve himself, of his own conviction that the ensuing battle would leave only a few survivors on the Persian side. Herodotus reports that he heard this story himself from Thersandros and adds that Thersandros had told the story to others in the days before the battle at Plataea. The source, the methodology and the resulting narrative all have the look of rock-solid adequacy: confidence is only slightly diminished when the Persian is said to have replied to Thersandros' suggestion that Mardonios be told of this by saying, 'What the god decides must happen no man can avert.' It looks very much as if Herodotus or Thersandros has coloured the remembered event with a tone that is entirely Greek, a possibility we need to keep in mind throughout Herodotus' work. But for the rest the story surely stands as it was told by Thersandros: it is a genuine testimony of how events surrounding the battle of Plataea were remembered.

Thersandros is typical of one sort of informant who regularly appears in Herodotus' work, a notable Greek or non-Greek with whom Herodotus has been able to establish some sort of personal connection. Another such is the Spartan Archias, whom Herodotus tells us (3.54–5) he met in Archias' home village of Pitane at Sparta. It was he who told Herodotus the story of how his grandfather, another Archias, had died a heroic death when he was surrounded, with a single companion, after they had broken into the acropolis of the Samians during an unsuccessful Spartan siege of the town of Samos. His grandfather had been given a public burial by the Samians as a mark of his courage, and the younger Archias' father had been named Samios in recognition of the honour in which his family held the people of Samos. The details of this story are circumstantial and the information attributed to Archias is not of great historical moment: there is no reason at all to doubt the authenticity of Herodotus' report of his source, and every reason to accept it. Not all of Herodotus' notable informants were Greek: he mentions (4.76) information he got about the family of the legendary Scythian sage, Anacharsis, from Tymnes, the agent of the Scythian king Ariapeithes;

Tymnes may very well have been a Carian, and Herodotus is likely to have met him in one of the Black Sea Greek colonies, perhaps Olbia in southern Russia.

Sometimes the encounter is clearly sought by Herodotus, as when he goes to Dodona in north-west Greece to ask about the origins of the oracle of Zeus there (2.55–7); he had been told in Egypt that this oracle had been founded by Egyptian priestesses carried off by Phoenician pirates. At Dodona he talks to the three priestesses of the sanctuary, whom he names and calls the 'spokeswomen' of the god, and to 'other Dodonans connected with the holy place', and he questions them about the traditions of their sanctuary. The tale they tell, which Herodotus takes to corroborate the Egyptian account, involves talking black doves who utter human speech: Herodotus interprets this as a folk-memory which has with time transformed unintelligible (because non-Greek) speech into the cooing of birds. His interpretation is explicitly his own but there are no good grounds for doubting his report of what he was told as local tradition.

The situation in which Herodotus put his questions to his informants was often, one may guess, that in which he himself imagines Greeks of the remoter past questioning and being questioned by men of power and status in the non-Greek world – for example, his story of Solon's stay as a guest in the palace of the Lydian king, Croesus (1.30.1–2). After two or three days of being entertained by the king, Solon is summoned by Croesus and questioned about his experiences before coming to Sardis. Earlier in the first book (1.27.2), Herodotus tells how another Greek (his sources disagreed as to whether it was Bias from Priene or Pittacus from Lesbos) was questioned by Croesus about the news from the Greek world: the connection between hospitality and the exchange of information is taken for granted by Herodotus. It is, of course, as old as Odysseus' visit to Phaeacia or that of Telemachus to the palace of Menelaus in the *Odyssey*, and it is almost certainly one model for Herodotus' own mode of enquiry, when he seeks information from men of the same rank as those he names in his narrative. If this is right, it will throw some light on the nature of the information Herodotus owes to such sources: the exchanges will have taken place within the social context of a bond of hospitality, and the information that Herodotus received is likely to reflect well on his host's ancestors. It is noticeable that in two of the cases in which he refers to his source by name the information he attributes to them is a matter of family tradition, and there are other cases of the kind.

It is very likely that Herodotus owes other such information to informants whom we can identify but whom he does not specifically name as his sources. He tells a memorable story (8.65, especially 65.6) of an uncanny event that occurred on the plain of Eleusis in the days before the battle of Salamis, when the countryside of Attica had been abandoned by its inhabitants, an event which was witnessed, Herodotus asserts, by only two people. The one he names as the source of the story is an Athenian political exile named Dikaios who had gained considerable status with the Persians; but he does not say that he had himself heard the story directly from Dikaios. The other witness is the deposed Spartan king, Demaratus, who had also been accepted as a friend by the Persian king, Dareius, and had been given land by him in the Troad within the Persian empire, where his son and grandson lived after him. The probability is that Herodotus had talked to both men, or more likely to their descendants. Demaratus figures as a central character in more than half a dozen stories told by Herodotus, several of which involve private conversations between Demaratus and a member of the Persian royal family: in almost all of them Demaratus plays a conspicuously admirable role. His advice is proved right, even when it is rejected, and Herodotus strikingly accepts an explanation of the appalling suicide which tradition recorded of the Spartan king, Kleomenes, which sees its cause in Kleomenes' role in the deposition and exile of Demaratus. It looks very much as if we should see the source of these stories and opinions in some member of Demaratus' family, even though Herodotus himself never claims to have spoken to any of them.

Even more striking is the case of another exile. The Persian Zopyros, whose father Megabyxos commanded one of the infantry divisions in Xerxes' great expeditionary force of 480 BC, was an exile in Athens at some time in the mid-fifth century. Several incidents in the history of Zopyros' family figure prominently in Herodotus' narrative, among them the bizarre story (3.160.2) of Zopyros' grandfather, another Zopyros, who was singlehandedly responsible for the capture of Babylon by a brilliant and courageous stratagem, after the armies of Dareius had besieged it without success for more than a year and a half. Herodotus records Dareius' undying gratitude to the elder Zopyros in extravagant terms. He had an earlier reason to be grateful: the elder Zopyros had been one of the seven conspirators who carried out the coup which put Dareius on the Persian throne. Herodotus' account of that episode is given in great detail and, we shall see, is supported at several points by Persian evidence in the form of Dareius' own inscriptions: it is probable that the younger Zopyros was one of his sources for that story, as also for the story (4.43.2) of how his aunt was raped by a nephew of Dareius, who was sent as punishment on an expedition to circumnavigate Africa and when he failed was impaled by his cousin, the then Persian king, Xerxes.

Everything points to the conclusion that these are events recorded in the traditions of particular great families and collected by Herodotus in the course of his enquiries. We have already encountered another very different kind of tradition which Herodotus also collected with equally passionate commitment, that of the priests and other officials at the holy places of the Mediterranean world. Apart from the priestesses at Dodona, Herodotus speaks of information he has had from the priests of Morduk at Babylon, from those of Melqaart at Tyre and from those of several gods at Memphis, Thebes and Sais in Egypt: we can probably add Akeratos, the 'spokesman' of Apollo at Delphi whom Herodotus names as sole witness of the miracles that happened at Delphi when the Persians came. On more than a dozen occasions in Books Two and Three Herodotus mentions Egyptian priests as his source, and attributes to them information not only about Egyptian history, both recent and long past, but also about the origins of Greek religion and about Paris, Helen and the Trojan War, for some of which the priests cited Menelaus as the ultimate source of their traditions. It seems also clear that a lot of what Herodotus reports about the behaviour of Cambyses in Egypt he owes to the Egyptian priesthood: some of it is demonstrably false, and Cambyses seems to have had his actions and character systematically blackened by the priests because he took away some of their previous rights and privileges.[3]

Herodotus' use of information, which he tells us comes from non-Greek sources such as the priests of Egyptian temples, clearly raises a question of linguistic comprehension on which we could do with being better informed. It is almost certain that Herodotus did not know enough of any language other than Greek to be able to communicate without the need of interpreters. He quite definitely knows of the use of interpreters: they figure as a separate class in his account of Egyptian society, and he traces their origins to a deliberate act by the sixth-century pharaoh Psammetichos to have a number of Egyptian boys taught Greek by Ionian Greek mercenaries whom he had settled at Daphne near the Nile delta. Herodotus also records the presence of Greek-speaking interpreters on two occasions at the court of the Persian king (3.38.4; 3.140.3); in both cases, it is implied that Greeks could not communicate with Persians without them. Herodotus even has interpreters act as intermediaries in the conversation he reports (1.86) between Cyrus the Great and Croesus the Lydian king after the latter had been taken prisoner, though they disappear from the story almost immediately it is under way. Unfortunately, the only place where Herodotus refers to his own use of interpreters is in a passage in which, if anything is clear, it is that he has been misinformed, or has misunderstood or misremembered what he has been told (2.125.6): he tells us that 'the intepreter who was reading off the Egyptian script' of the inscription on the pyramid of Cheops informed him, 'to the best of my recollection', that 1,600 silver talents had been spent on 'radishes, onions and leeks' for the work force. Herodotus is astounded, as well he might have been: the total reserves of the Athenian treasury at the outbreak of the Peloponnesian War amounted to only some 6,000–9,000 talents. Astronomical sums, it must have seemed to Herodotus, would have been needed to pay for the full cost of the food, clothing and equipment required to complete the job.

Herodotus will certainly have been able to conduct his enquiries through Persian-speaking Greeks in the Persian capital; we have independent evidence for Greeks in the service of the Persian king, some of them in positions close to the highest Persian officials. One of these last is Parnaka, the uncle of Dareius and father of one of Xerxes' generals in 480 BC, known to Herodotus as Pharnakes: his son commanded the escort of 60,000 that accompanied Xerxes on his journey back into Asia after the defeat of Salamis. One of Pharnakes' aides at Persepolis was a man called in the Persian documents Yauna, almost certainly a Greek slave called by his ethnic rather than his unpronounceable Greek name.[4] Contacts between Greeks and the Persian king go back to the early years of Cyrus the Great when a Greek from Cyzicus, Pytharchus, was given several towns by the Persian king; Greek craftsmen later worked to build Cyrus' tomb at Pasargadae.

In the north, Herodotus himself reports (4.24) that he was able to get information about the peoples beyond the Black Sea not only from Greeks established at a trading post on the Dnieper and at the other Black Sea ports, but also from Scythians who carried on their dealings with the tribes of the interior in seven different languages by the use of interpreters.

Herodotus' own qualities of mind clearly protected him from the worst kind of insular non-comprehension of the real differences which separated him as a Greek from the non-Greeks with whom he had to deal. He does not show himself an easy prey to the complacent insularity to which Professor Momigliano has drawn our attention, and shown to be characteristic of so much in Greek relations with alien cultures. But how much was lost in the process of translation from one language and one culture to another is altogether a different question. It is only after more than half a century of anthropological fieldwork that we are beginning to get some idea of just how much misunderstanding is likely to occur when the preconceptions of one culture come face to face with those of another. The problem is more complicated than it might appear. It is not just that each party conducts its part in the encounter in terms of its own general understanding of the world, but also that each, questioner and questioned, confronts and addresses the other, and interprets his words and actions, in the light of a stereotyped 'knowledge' of the person addressed. Nigel Barley's Dowayo tribesmen well illustrate the point: they 'knew' that all white men were really black but had managed to cover their black skin with an outer skin of white which they stripped off at night behind locked doors and drawn curtains: this after all 'explained' why white men were so obsessed with privacy. White men were also 'known' to be 'really' reincarnated spirits of long-dead Dowayo sorcerers: it followed that Barley's struggles with the Dowayo language were an elaborate but pointless pretence aimed at disguising his true Dowayo nature.[5]

Cultural misunderstanding will certainly have occurred between Herodotus and his non-Greek informants: it will have been at its most severe, and most difficult to diagnose, when language was being used for symbolic purposes. The boundaries between literal and symbolic meaning will be peculiarly hard for a non-native speaker to discern, and here we should expect to find confusion and misunderstanding. Herodotus reports (1.136.2; 1.138.1) both that Persian boys were taught three things only: to ride, to use a bow and arrows and to tell the truth; and that lying was considered the most shaming thing a man could do, only followed by the shame of owing money, which in turn owed its shamefulness to the fact that it led to the telling of lies. This view of Persian education was all but universal among Greeks and other non-Persians: a Lycian tyrant of Xanthos put up an inscription in Greek verse recording his claim to know 'what wise men know: archery, virtue and hunting on horseback' (SEG 28.1245, ll. 14ff). But Herodotus' narrative itself does not suggest in the least that Persians avoided lying as the worst of human failings: the ruse of Zopyros by which the capture of Babylon was secured, Dareius' lie which was to give him admission to the throne-room of the usurper king, the

26

trap that the satrap Oroetes set for Polycrates of Samos, the affair of Xerxes with his brother's wife – all these are classic examples of lies told by Persians, in no way less striking than the lying stratagems Herodotus attributes to Greeks. It has been suggested that Herodotus and other Greeks misunderstood the use by their Persian sources of the phrase 'of the lie' to refer to the manifestations of the power of evil in its eternal struggle with Ahura Mazda, and in particular to those enemies of the Persian king who were seen as the agents of that power, such as the 'kings of the lie', the leaders of revolt against Persian power that Dareius claimed to have conquered in the first years of his reign.[6] The suggestion is that Herodotus has confused this symbolic use of the idea of 'the lie' with lying in the literal sense. He may well have made the same kind of mistake in treating the Persian king's use of terms like 'bondsman' to refer to .his subjects, even members of his own family, as if it implied the literal status of a slave: he uses the language of Greek chattel slavery and imagines Persian troops being whipped into action, crossing into Europe and digging the canal through Athos under whips (7.103.4; 7.223.3; 7.56.1; 7.22.1; for the implications of whipping, see 4.3.3–4).

Throughout Herodotus repeatedly refers to himself as 'hearing' the evidence on which his narrative is based (1.20; 2.29.1; 2.52.1; 2.148.6; 3.117.6; 4.14.1; 4.16.2, etc.), and to his informants as 'saying': 'he said', 'they say', 'it is said'. Three times he talks of his sources as *logioi*, 'those with something to say', 'those with a story to tell', 'those who know the stories': in the last instance these are equated with 'those who made a practice of the memory of the past' (1.1.1; 2.3.1; 2.77.1). It is clear that we are dealing with an oral tradition, and with those who keep it, and in order to grasp the nature of Herodotus' data it is to the characteristics of such traditions and to their variety that we need to turn.

If we are now in a position to understand something of the workings of oral tradition, to an extent that would have been impossible even a generation ago, it is largely due to the pioneering work of primary analysis done by scholars such as Jan Vansina and Ruth Finnegan, and to the work of Jack Goody and others on the changes of mental attitude brought about by the transition to literacy.[7] To Vansina in particular we owe an understanding of the enormous variety of different types of oral tradition and of the very different conditions in which they have been transmitted. This is important for an understanding of Herodotus, because if anything is clear it is that the traditions on which he was drawing were themselves quite disparate and that they exhibit quite different characteristics. In the very recent past historians and anthropologists have begun to investigate what they term 'social memory' and the characteristics of the collective memory of the past; this too helps to throw light on the narrative that Herodotus constructed on the basis of such data.[8]

We have already met Herodotus drawing on information gained from talking to aristocratic informants about the family traditions which they had inherited about the deeds of their own ancestors. We have independent evidence for the existence of quite long chains of genealogical tradition within wealthy families in the Greek world: an inscription from Chios, for example, on a tombstone of the mid-fifth century, records fifteen generations of the male ancestry of the dead man, Heropythos, and gives the name of each of his ancestors in the male line. A striking feature of the family traditions used by Herodotus is the dazzling light of approval in which the actions of the ancestor or ancestors in question are almost always seen – hardly surprising in view of the interests which such traditions exist to serve. Herodotus' readiness to accept the truthfulness of such traditions must almost certainly stem from his own assessment of the credibility of his informant, a personal judgment certainly liable to error but over which we can exercise no control. Perhaps it also involved a more general assumption of trustworthiness in men of the social rank of informants such as Zopyros or Demaratus: the status of the story derives from the status of the family.

A quite different form of tradition used much more frequently by Herodotus and one which he seems to accept on quite different grounds, is the traditional tale informally current in a particular local community: here Herodotus' method

of assessing the accuracy of the information he received seems
to have been to check stories that he has heard in one local
community with those current in another, and to incline to
believe those he heard in more than one such locality. These
are the tales which he attributes to 'the Corinthians', 'the
Athenians', 'the men of Delphi', 'the men of Metapontum'
and the like. His informants are anonymous, collective,
clearly distinguished from the aristocratic witnesses for whom
he gives names and patronymics. These are traditions shared
by the whole community: as the Spartan king Leotychidas
says to the Athenian assembly, 'We Spartans have a story
. . .' (6.86a, 2). In one particularly instructive case, Herodotus
refers to these tales as told by 'the towns' in question. This
last is the story of Aristeas in Book Four (4.14–15), and is
a good example of Herodotus' attitude to such tales. He begins
by saying that the story is one he 'heard in the towns of Proconessos and Cyzicus', two Greek communities on the sea of
Marmara, some forty miles apart: one on the mainland, the
other an island town. It is the story of Aristeas' disappearance,
his reappearance six years later and second disappearance
from his home town of Proconessos, given in circumstantial
detail which includes some degree of local knowledge; Herodotus' silence suggests that the version current in one town
was no different from that in the other. He goes on to add
a kind of coda to the story which involves a further miraculous
reappearance of Aristeas, this time more than six hundred
miles away even as the crow flies, at Metapontum in southern
Italy, where, Herodotus tells us, he heard the story at a date
which he calculates, 'putting together what I discovered at
Proconessos and at Metapontum', to be 240 years after Aristeas' second disappearance. Throughout Herodotus tells the
story in the form of reported speech. The impression left is
of a careful comparison of traditions current in different local-
ities and the acceptance of the resulting testimony on the
grounds of its (presumed) independent existence in more than
one community (4.14–15). We can see Herodotus using the
same method of assessment in his story of the miraculous
rescue of Arion from drowning by a dolphin: he attributes
the story (again told in reported speech) to 'the Corinthians',

and comments that 'the men of Lesbos tell the same story': at the end of his report of the tale he adds that 'there is a small bronze statue of a man on a dolphin, dedicated by Arion, at Cape Taenarum in the Peloponnese', where the story said that Arion was brought to shore by the dolphin. The coincidence of these different testimonies seems to have been enough in itself to convince Herodotus of the truth of a story involving abnormal, not to say supernatural, experiences: the possibility that the same folk-motif might arise independently in more than one place did not occur to him. It was perhaps the absence of corroboration that led him to reject stories less obviously fantastic, such as that of Skyllias of Skione. The story that Herodotus heard was that Skyllias, 'the finest diver of that time', who deserted from the Persian fleet when it was anchored off the north coast of Euboea and made his way across to the Greek fleet on the island, had swum under water all the way across the strait to Artemisium, a distance that Herodotus calculates as ten miles. 'I cannot say for certain', he writes, 'how he reached the Greeks but I should be surprised if the story told about him is true. ... There are other stories told about this man that look as if they are fictions, though among them there are true stories. On this point I should declare my belief that he reached Artemisium in a boat' (8.8.1–3). Skyllias, presumably, was a man about whom tall stories were told.

Some of these traditions may be very much of the locality, with no wider currency: Herodotus himself stresses the purely 'local' nature of the tradition about the temple of Zeus Laphystios at Halos on the gulf of Pagasae and the descendants of the legendary Athamas, with its implications of human sacrifice, which local guides told to Xerxes (7.197.1–4). Herodotus shows himself well aware too that there are limits to the reach of the oral traditions on which he was able to draw, so that there may be events and places at a remoter distance in time or space to which his sources could not give him access: the Carians, he reports, had not paid tribute, even to Minos, 'ever, as far as I have been able to reach in what I have heard', and there must be places, such as the sources of the Nile or the remoter tribes of the Scythians, which his 'enquiry' cannot reveal: as he acknowledges, he can only report 'as far as I have been able to reach in my enquiries', 'in what I have heard' (1.171.2; 2.34.1: cf. 2.29.1; 4.16.2). He is aware too that the memory of events may be lost to the tradition: twice he records that a detail (the replies of the oracles other than Delphi to Croesus; the division of the spoils after Plataea) 'is not told by anyone' (1.147.2; 9.81.2). When he encounters conflicting traditions he is sensitive to the kinds of interested distortion that may occur. The Spartans sent (1.70) a huge bronze *krater* to Croesus as a gift which never reached Sardis; Herodotus had seen it as a dedication in the sanctuary of Hera on Samos. There were two contradictory accounts of its fate: in Sparta the story was that it had been stolen by Samians while in Samian waters; on Samos Herodotus heard a different story, that the Spartans taking it to Croesus had been too dilatory, and that Sardis had fallen to the Persians before the *krater* arrived; it had been sold to private buyers on Samos who had then dedicated it to Hera. Herodotus' comment on these conflicting versions, which are told in indirect speech, is given in his own person: 'it is likely enough that the men who had sold it would say, when they got back to Sparta, that they had been robbed of it by Samians'. Certainly divergence within a tradition is a common enough feature, and it can produce stories so different that their common starting-point may be almost entirely lost sight of. The process is well illustrated by the tradition about Gyges, the first of the Mermnad kings of Lydia, a certainly historical figure whose seizure of the Lydian throne dates from the end of the eighth century BC. In Herodotus (1.8–13) his story is the story of the infatuation of his predecessor Kandaules: of how Kandaules obliged Gyges to see what he should not have seen, Kandaules' wife naked in her own bedroom, and how Kandaules' wife in her turn compelled Gyges to assassinate her husband in his bed in revenge for her humiliation and to become king of Lydia in turn as her husband. Little more than a century after Herodotus, the story of Gyges reappears in Plato: by now Gyges is a man who becomes king of Lydia through being unseen; he becomes possessor of a ring of invisibility when the ground opens in front of him as he watches over the king's sheep and reveals a grave with a gigantic skeleton in it; with the ring taken from the grave the unseen Gyges seduces the king's wife and murders her husband to become king in his place (Plato, *Republic* 2.359d–360b). Scholars have thought that the two men called Gyges must be different: it is only when we notice the common structural motifs of seen/unseen and the supplanting of the king as husband as well as ruler that we perceive both stories as traditional versions of the same event, the overthrow of the Heraklid kings of Lydia. Herodotus, familiar with the workings of an oral tradition, is likely to have found such divergence altogether less surprising or misleading than we do.[9]

But there are other characteristics of these collective tales to which Herodotus shows himself much less sensitive, above all their tendency to become accommodated to stereotyped patterns, to follow a logic of traditional 'motifs' which can be transferred from one tale to another. They are familiar to us from other traditional tales which we tend to call rather 'myths' or 'folk-tales'. Significantly, perhaps, since it concerns the childhood of a great historical figure, and one about whom Herodotus feels confident that he has accurate information, one of the best examples of this tendency is in his account of the birth and upbringing of Cyrus the Great. Here (1.95.1) he records that he could tell three versions of the story other than the one he chooses to tell, which he attributes to unidentified 'Persians', describing them only as 'those who do not set out to make the story of Cyrus awesome but to tell the true tale'. Herodotus' 'true tale' involves two dreams prophetic of his overthrow dreamed by the Median king Astyages; the consequent exposure of his grandchild, his daughter's son, who, the dreams foretell, will supplant him; the rescue of the child through the agency of Harpagus, the man entrusted with its exposure; the discovery, years later, of the true identity of the child; and Astyages' revenge on Harpagus by butchering his son and serving the flesh to him unrecognized at a feast. The similarities with what we would call the myths of Paris and Oedipus, for example, as well as with Near Eastern stories of Moses, Gilgamesh and Sargon, and with the mythical revenge of Atreus on Thyestes and that of Procne and Philomela on Tereus, are immediately striking, but they did not deter Herodotus from recording this as the version of Cyrus' origins that had the best claim to be accepted as true. It is a measure of the difficulties that *we* have in coming to terms with the oral tradition on which Herodotus draws that it is with a shock that we encounter the same Harpagus, eater of his own son's flesh, as the general in command of the Persian army which carried out the certainly historical subjection of the Ionian Greek cities in about 540 BC (1.162ff.) Similar 'mythologizing' motifs occur repeatedly elsewhere in the local traditions from which Herodotus derives his narrative: the prophecy of overthrow and the attempt to avoid it by exposing the endangering child reappears in the birth-story of Kypselos, subsequently the tyrant of Corinth; the cannibalistic revenge in the story of the revenge of the Scythian nomads on the Median king, Kyaxares (5.92.2ff.; 1.73.4–6).[10]

Other stories that Herodotus encountered display features that we know from stories of the folk-tale or märchen type, familiar to us through such collections as the Grimm brothers. In Book Eight (8.137–9) Herodotus tells the story of the founding of the Macedonian royal dynasty, as he almost certainly heard it in Macedon itself. Three brothers, descendants of the Argive king, Temenos, arrived in the town of Lebaia in upper Macedonia and began working as hired hands of the local 'king': the eldest looked after the horses, the second the cattle and the youngest the smaller animals. The king's wife herself baked the bread for the three brothers; she noticed that the loaf she made for the youngest every time doubled in size, and told her husband of this. He recognized that this was an omen 'and meant some big thing'. Summoning the brothers, he told them to leave his country. They replied that they would leave when they had been paid the wages they were entitled to. The sun was shining through the chimney hole on to the floor of the room; hearing the brothers' reply the king pointed to the sunlight and said, 'This is the wage you deserve and this I give to you': a god had turned his mind. Two of the brothers stood dumbfounded, but the youngest, with a sword in his hand, said, 'We accept what you give us, sire,' and drew round the patch of sunlight on the floor. So doing, he drew the sunlight three times into the fold of his tunic, and left the house with his brothers. The king, warned by a bystander what this meant, sent off men on horseback to kill the three brothers. The brothers had just crossed a nearby river when a sudden flood made it impossible for their pursuers to get across, and the brothers survived and prospered in another part of Macedonia, where roses with sixty petals and a scent that surpasses all others grow. There they were safe and eventually they came back and made themselves masters of the whole of Macedonia. In this story, not only the motif of the youngest son but also marking out the sunlight with a sword as a claim to rights of ownership, the doubling in size of the loaves of bread, the sudden spate of the river that thwarts the pursuers, and the inserted detail of the roses with sixty petals are features that could be paralleled in the stories collected by the Grimm brothers.[11]

Most surprising, perhaps, in what we can call the 'mythologizing' assimilation of tradition to the patterns of the storyteller is the speed with which the process operates. The fall of Sardis and the advance of Persian power under Cyrus to the Aegean coast were events of not much more than a century before Herodotus was collecting the traditions about them, but already these traditions have undergone a quite radical assimilation. In the case of the traditions about Croesus, we can, as it happens, trace something of the way in which the process takes place. Already before 500 BC – that is, little more than a generation after the fall of Sardis – the fame of Croesus was widespread in the Greek world, including the mainland of Greece itself: a rich Athenian had already named his son Croesus by the early 520s at the latest as we know from the statue (now in the National Museum at Athens) which he set up over his son's grave some time before 500.[12] Soon after that, an Athenian vase painter had painted a scene of Croesus on the pyre on a red-figure amphora now in the Louvre. The tradition on which the painter was drawing looks to have been very different from Herodotus': Croesus is enthroned on the pyre, wreathed and holding a sceptre in his left hand while with his right he pours a libation on to the pyre; a slave, named Euthymos on the vase, is lighting the pyre. The whole scene appears to be one of sacrifice, an act of ritual self-immolation, not unlike the story of ritual suicide on a funeral pyre that Herodotus tells of Adrastus (1.45.1–3). It may be significant that Herodotus knows of two other stories of the self-immolation of non-Greeks: the suicide of Bogas, the Persian governor of Eion in Thrace, and that of the Carthaginian 'king', Hamilcar (7.107; 7.166–7). Self-immolation may be another recurrent motif of the storyteller: these stories refer to events of 480 BC or later, and the second of them has all the hallmarks of a 'miracle' tale of 'the man who disappeared' (it is attributed to 'the Carthaginians', but Herodotus comments that it is likely to be true). In 468 BC the Greek poet Bacchylides wrote a victory-song for Hieron, the tyrant of Syracuse in Sicily, in which the story of Croesus is told as a paradigm of the holy man miraculously rescued by the gods and carried away to the magical land of the Hyperboreans in the face of certain death; two years earlier another Greek poet, Pindar, could refer in passing, as if to something that his audience would immediately recognize and respond to, to the 'kindly excellence' of Croesus 'which does not die'. By 470, clearly, Croesus is already a legendary figure for all his historical reality.

Other events still closer in date to Herodotus' own enquiries show signs of the same process. Herodotus knows of a story told by one of the Athenians who fought in the battle of Marathon, in 490 BC, of how he found himself confronting, during the course of the battle, an apparition of an armed man of great height whose beard cast a shadow over his entire shield and who bypassed him but killed the man fighting next to him in the battle-line. The man who had the vision, whose name and patronymic Herodotus gives, went blind in the course of the battle and never recovered his sight. In this case Herodotus specifically does *not* claim to have heard his story at first hand, but twice says that he has heard that Epizelos himself 'used to tell' the story about the apparition (6.117.2–3). The blinding of Epizelos, we know, was also recorded in a famous painting of the battle of Marathon on the walls of the Stoa Poikile in Athens, executed only thirty years or so after the battle and almost certainly before Herodotus wrote his narrative (Pausanias 1.15.1–4; 1.21).[13] Long afterwards, the local tradition of the villagers of Marathon recorded other supernatural appearances during the battle, as well as uncanny sounds of horses whinnying and men shouting and fighting which could still be heard, centuries later, on the battlefield after dark, but we have no means of dating the origin of these traditions (Pausanias 1.32.3). Before the battle of Salamis, in 480 BC, we have the story of the ghostly procession across the plain of Eleusis, seen and heard by Dikaios and Demaratus, to which I have already referred; and on the day of the battle itself the supernatural vision of a ship and the sound of a voice coming from it that confronted the Corinthian admiral, Adeimantus, when, according to Athenian tradition, he attempted to flee before the battle was fully joined (8.65; 8.94).

We have to remember, of course, that stories of uncanny events surrounding great battles, or the birth and childhood of great men, are arguably a special case, both in the frequency of their occurrence and in the swiftness with which they appear in oral tradition: the story implying that Plato's father was really Apollo – his father dreamed that his wife would give birth to a child by the god – is attributed to Speusippus, Plato's own nephew (Diogenes Laertius 3.2: the story is said to be one told at Athens), and the battlefield vision of the angel of Mons, a conspicuous parallel to Epizelos' vision, is already attested within a year of the battle.[14]

Evidently the local traditions which Herodotus' enquiries revealed were already, within one or two generations of the events that they recorded, strongly affected by this process of 'mythologizing': in his narrative we everywhere get the feel, as he himself constantly reminds us, of what men actually said in his own lifetime, of how they remembered events in many of which their fathers and grandfathers had taken part. A large part of the imaginative hold which Herodotus has always exercised over his readers stems precisely from our sense of listening to how men spoke. Analogy with other, contemporary oral traditions suggests that such memories may be highly selective in what is recalled and spoken of:

what is remembered is what has significance in the world of the living and relates to the general experience of the community. It also suggests that the vividness of the memory is in itself no guarantee of historical authenticity, even when it is offered as the testimony of an eyewitness: one recent investigator was told by a man born in 1925 of the appearance of Turks as they 'strolled around the village' (a mountain village in central Greece which had seen no Turks since the mid-nineteenth century), and the same informant pointed to a plane tree under which he had seen 'a Turkish woman sitting on a swing, her eyes looking out from under her veil, the most beautiful woman in the world!' Nonetheless, such memories are accepted in the community as embodying the meaning of the past.[15]

Herodotus' own attitude to such memories is complex and not easily made out. Before we leave his account of the fall of Croesus and the Lydian kingdom, we should notice one striking fact about it that is often passed over. This is that, with the exception of one section, the whole narrative is (unusually) told in direct speech, in Herodotus' own person, and that only once does he identify the tradition or traditions on which he is drawing. The exception occurs precisely in the account of Croesus on the pyre (1.86). Herodotus records that it was Cyrus who had Croesus, bound and fettered, put on the pyre along with fourteen Lydian youths, and goes on to speculate on Cyrus' motives for this act: he entertains three possibilities. At this point the narrative suddenly, and without any verb of saying, goes into indirect speech; shortly afterwards, at the moment when Cyrus changes his mind and gives orders for the pyre to be put out and Croesus and those with him taken down from it, Herodotus records (1.86) that 'it is said by some Lydians' that Croesus at this moment, realizing that Cyrus had changed his mind, prayed aloud in tears to Apollo to rescue him in return for his many benefactions to the god, and that a sudden, violent downpour put out the pyre. That is to say, the only indication of his sources in oral tradition that Herodotus gives during his narrative of Croesus' downfall occurs at precisely the moment when we know independently from other sources that there were conflicting traditions; in this instance he claims to be drawing on stories current in Lydia itself for the episode of the miraculous intervention of the god. Despite this, scholars have confidently attributed the story of the miracle to priests of Apollo at Delphi or at Delos. Herodotus' silence elsewhere in the Croesus story as to his sources, we may guess, is the result of the wide diffusion of traditions about Croesus: the story was so widespread that Herodotus feels it unnecessary, or is unable, to name specific local traditions as the source of his narrative.

But Croesus is an exception. It is important that we should remind ourselves of the extent to which the vast majority of these oral traditions are of purely local currency, because otherwise we shall not come near to taking the measure of Herodotus' originality, nor understand the truly daunting nature of the task he set himself. It is an essential part of the function of the 'social memory' on which Herodotus draws that it should serve to maintain the solidarity of the local community and the distinctive nature of its experience. We have recently been reminded by Simon Hornblower how small the local community of fifth-century Greece typically is, how narrow the distance separating one community from the next and how strong the sense of difference and mutual enmity between neighbours which supported the community's sense of identity and distinctiveness.[16] A community's traditions will often have had no value outside its own borders, and will often have encountered a contrary tradition in the very next community: 'the *polis* next door was another world'. Thus the Greek world (as we see it) will have contained a myriad of separate and different 'social memories' enshrined in oral tradition. Even if it was part of 'Xerxes' legacy', to use Hornblower's phrase, to have created, for a time, a new and powerful sense of common Greekness among the Greek communities, that does not lessen Herodotus' achievement, which was to have caught the sense of that common Greekness and turned local memory into universal narrative. For Herodotus' 'enquiries' had, or came to have, as their object to enable him to construct an inclusive narrative of the process by which 'Greeks and Persians came into conflict with one another', a narrative in which the heroic actions and achievements of men remembered only within the local community would have their due place as part of a single experience, 'the Persian wars'. His achievement is precisely to have created such a story; not just to have recorded 'what was said' in this or the other community by Athenians or Corinthians or Lydians or Egyptians, but to have made out of such 'saying' a single narrative of what a whole generation of men remembered.

A final feature of the oral traditions that are Herodotus' material calls for some comment. The traditions that become stereotyped in the forms we call myth or folk-tale tend to detach themselves from any reference to temporal sequence which would make it possible to fit them into a chronological scheme in which they could figure in some sense alongside the audience's own experience of the present: 'once upon a time', they begin, or in Greek stories, 'there was once a time . . .'. But Herodotus' stories are, for the most part, anchored somewhere in a single continuum of time, either by counting years or more often by counting generations.[17] The story of the three brothers, the youngest of whom became the first king of Macedonia, does not happen 'once upon a time' but is located by Herodotus in the sixth generation before the Alexander, son of Amyntas, who was used by the Persians in the winter of 480–79 BC to negotiate with Athens, and Herodotus gives the names of Alexander's ancestors in each generation back to the Perdiccas who was the 'youngest brother' of the story (8.139). Similarly, the tale of Glaucus that Leotychidas told at Athens, which begins 'we Spartans have a story . . .', goes on, 'two generations before my time' (6.86.2).

In two separate places Herodotus gives the ancestry of the two Spartan kings most prominent in the war with Persia, Leonidas and Leotychidas, in twenty generations in each case back to Herakles, naming the ancestry of each (7.204; 8.131.2), and long stretches of time are regularly recorded by a count of generations. Thus four generations separate Croesus from Gyges (1.13.2; 1.91.1); eight generations fall between the Spartan colonists who refounded Thera from the first settlement by the nephew of Cadmus the Phoenician (4.147.5), and eight generations is the predicted length of the reign of the Battiad kings of Cyrene given to Arkesilas by the Pythia at Delphi (4.163.2). Twice a calculation in generations is turned into a count of years: once for the length of the rule of the Heraklid kings of Lydia (1.7.4), where twenty-two generations is given alternatively as 505 years; and a second time when Herodotus calculates what he takes to be the recorded genealogy of the kings of Egypt as 340 generations, or 11,340 years. On this last occasion, he offers a conversion formula (three human generations equals a hundred years) and we can see that his calculation is faulty or his copyists in error. There is argument among scholars as to the source or sources from which Herodotus derives his chronological data. Jack Goody has pointed out that the making of lists of all kinds is a characteristic phenomenon of the first impact of literacy on an oral culture,[18] and it may be that Herodotus' information on chronology comes from lists made first from oral tradition by his predecessor, Hecataeus of Miletus. A calculation by generations is clearly the base for Herodotus' chronology: the nine hundred years that Herodotus calculates for the lapse of time that separates him from Herakles, and the four hundred years that he believes have passed between the time of Homer and Hesiod and his own life time could both be easily arrived at by converting generations into centuries (2.145.4; 2.53.2). In the second case Herodotus is, perhaps surprisingly, quite emphatic that Homer and Hesiod did not live any earlier than his own calculations suggested: in this he is perhaps drawing on the traditions of the so-called Homeridae ('descendants of Homer'), the guild of performers of epic poetry that existed on Chios, who are likely to have maintained their own genealogy, claiming descent from Homer himself.

At all events, Herodotus' ability to think readily and fluently in terms of kinship and generations, and his use of these structures to map the past, not just within the history of individual families but across whole communities and peoples and their interrelationships, is another facet of his familiarity with the form of human social memory embodied in oral tradition. That is a familiarity we have lost and which was soon to disappear from the world of ancient Greece. Another observation reinforces the point. Two of the most memorable of Herodotus' traditional tales, the story of Glaucus the Spartan and the birth story of Kypselos, tyrant of Corinth, are told in the course of speeches by envoys of major cities to mass assemblies, as a means of persuading them to political decisions (6.86; 5.92). We have only to look forward a generation to the work of Thucydides, Herodotus' successor, to see how unthinkable by then was the very idea of telling a story to support a political argument. Herodotus' world is still the world of the teller of tales, from king to shepherd. A generation later storytelling has come to seem naive and is no longer an accepted means of persuasion in the public arena of political debate and argument; a generation later still, Plato can refer to traditional tales dismissively as the 'wittering of old women', 'old wives' tales' (Plato, *Theaetetus* 176b). That shift in perception is not a gain; it does not represent progress from 'primitive' to 'modern' conceptions of historical thinking. Rather, to paraphrase James Redfield, Herodotus' conception of historical thought as embodied in traditional stories 'raises (rather than lowers) the level of reasoning'.[19]

3 The Logic of
Narrative

Herodotus' language is lucid and his sentences have a natural relaxed rhythm and scale, a natural speakability. The narrative has a similar appearance of lucidity as it leads from the confrontation between Cyrus and Croesus to the great invasion of Xerxes. But to confront the detail of Herodotean narrative, to attempt to grasp its scale and shape and see order in the mass, is a mind-blowing and overwhelming experience. The first impression one has is of being buried under an avalanche of facts and at the same time utterly lost in a landscape bewilderingly criss-crossed and looped by stories without discernible paths or sense of structured connection. Structure, except on the very largest scale, is at first invisible. Moreover, the world that Herodotus makes is peopled by an enormous multitude of individuals: a rather rough and ready count of the personal names in Herodotus (making use of Enoch Powell's *Lexicon*) suggests that there are over 940 named individuals who appear as characters in the world of this story. That fact is itself perhaps the first clue to structure. To grasp the importance of the personal is the key to one aspect of Herodotean story-telling. Connection in Herodotus' narrative is everywhere made by personal relationships, through the interconnections of individuals or communities, by kinship ties and also by ties of reciprocal obligation whether of repaying good by good or of revenge for hurt, and by the complementary relationships of aggressor and victim (or intended victim) or of donor and recipient of gifts. What ties the history of Athens and Sparta into Herodotus' narrative at their first appearance is Croesus' enquiries into the relative strengths of different Greek cities so that he might find, as the Delphic oracle had instructed him to do, 'the most powerful of the Greeks' and make them his 'friends' (1.53.3) – that is, construct a new tie with them by giving and receiving gifts. Kinship, and the twin obligations of repaying favours and exacting revenge, provide the subtext of connections which at the same time constitute both a chronological framework through the mapping of generations (since both obligations can be inherited), and a framework of explanation, as we shall see in the next chapter. The further ties established by aggression and gift-giving extend the range of connection and bring together parties not previously related, without seeming of themselves to require further explanation. Reciprocal obligation as a principle of exchange in the sense defined by Marcel Mauss in his classic *Essai sur le don*[1] is enacted in the exchange of gifts, and significantly Herodotus' narrative includes a prodigious repertoire of gifts given and received, embracing alike the gifts of man to man and of man to god, all in detail recorded and their histories traced.[2] Gift-giving is one aspect of the institution known to ancient Greeks as *xenia*, a word which defies easy translation into English: its most recent student has called it 'ritualized friendship'.[3] The obligations of *xenia*, along with those of kinship, form one of the most powerful strands of connection which structure Herodotus' narrative, but it remains barely visible since it is something which he and his readers take for granted.

Anyone with knowledge of contemporary Mediterranean and in particular Greek society and its habit of extending kinship obligations by relationships of hospitality or by the more formalized institution of the *koumbaros* ('godfather' is a familiar but not an altogether satisfactory translation) will find these things the less surprising. What Herodotus does is simply to extend the model of personal relationships, based on kinship and *xenia*, gratitude, and revenge, familiar to everyone in his audience in the small world of their own everyday experience, until it embraces the whole world of narrative opened up by his enquiries, the 'historical world' that constitutes his subject. By comparison, analogical relationships – that is, relationships derived from perceived connections between abstractions, such as ones between the behaviour of otherwise unconnected 'tyrants' – are much less significant. To quote a British anthropologist once more, this time

E.E.Evans-Pritchard on the perception of time by the Nuer, a Nilotic people whose culture he analysed in three exemplary monographs: 'Beyond the annual cycle, time-reckoning is a conceptualization of the social structure, and the points for reference are a projection into the past of actual relationships between persons. It is less a means of co-ordinating events than of co-ordinating relationships, and is therefore mainly a looking-backwards, since relationships must be explained in terms of the past.'[4] As we shall see in the following chapter, the structure of obligations which underlies Herodotus' text also serves to relate his narrative to the most powerful explanatory model of experience possessed by ancient Greeks, the model of reciprocating action. From the 'anger of Achilles' in the *Iliad* to the definition of justice offered by Polemarchus in the first book of Plato's *Republic*, the model of repayment in kind is perceived as the most serious account available of human behaviour, and as capable of extension beyond that to embrace the nature of extra-human experience as well.

To illustrate the application of this model to Herodotean narrative, let us look at Herodotus' account of the process by which the Persians conquered the Lydian kingdom and thus, for the first time, came into contact with the Greek cities of the Aegean coast. Cyrus is urged by Harpagus the Mede to take revenge on Astyages, his maternal grandfather, for his attempt to have Cyrus killed as an infant; in the process Harpagus also obtains revenge on Astyages for having his son killed and his flesh served to him as food. The double revenge of Cyrus and Harpagus involves making the Persians rise against the Medes, their overlords, and ends with Cyrus established as king of the Medes and Persians. In turn it provides the motive of revenge for Croesus, the Lydian king and brother-in-law of Astyages, to attack Cyrus and the Persians, an act which, by miscalculation, results in his own overthrow and in the kingdom of Lydia passing into the control of Persia. These events, which form the starting-point of Herodotus' narrative of the history of conflict between Greeks and Persians, are anchored to the 'present' of Herodotus' story and its audience by being attached to the person of the predecessor of the Persian king Xerxes, who led the great invasion of

Greece in 480 BC, three generations later. Though Cyrus was not in fact Xerxes' great-grandfather in the male line, a cognatic link is made by the marriage of Xerxes' father Dareius' to Atossa, the daughter of Cyrus and the sister as well as the wife of Cambyses, Dareius' predecessor as king of Persia, and by his making her the mother of Xerxes. Moreover, in the cause of recording the stories of Croesus and Cyrus up to the point of their confrontation, Herodotus has included genealogies and abbreviated histories of the Lydian kings (the ancestors of Croesus) and of the kings of Media (the ancestors of Astyages), as well as accounts of Athenian and Spartan history (as potential 'friends' of Croesus) and a number of other subordinate stories (those of Solon and Adrastus, for example), tied into the main narrative by connections of hospitality and religious obligation ('supplication').[5]

I have so far left out of account one obvious and highly significant fact about Herodotus' telling of the stories of Croesus and Cyrus, and that is that they are not told in chronological sequence. Herodotus begins with Croesus, backtracks to his great-great-grandfather Gyges, brings the story down through four generations once more to Croesus, mentions in passing the overthrow of Astyages by Cyrus, continues with the account of Croesus' attack on the Persians (including the digression on Athens and Sparta), describes how Astyages came to marry the sister of Croesus, completes the story of Croesus' downfall, and only then reverts to the birth and childhood of Cyrus, prefacing that story with the accounts of Cyrus' maternal great-great-great-grandfather, his great-great-grandfather, his great-grandfather and his grandfather. The present-day reader is likely to be already reeling from encountering a story in which a (to him) largely invisible genealogical structure has replaced the chronological sequence which is now expected in historical narrative: passing allusions (as to the fact that Croesus' father fought a war against the Medes under Cyrus' maternal great-grandfather, referred to as the 'grandson of Deioces') are almost bound to escape notice altogether. What these things demonstrate is the capacity of Herodotus and his audience to think more or less instinctively in terms of relationships which for us

45

have to be elaborately reconstructed and committed to writing as a 'family tree' before they can be raised to consciousness and begin to make sense, and which even then do not in any real sense structure our experience of the past. It is not surprising that we have difficulties with Herodotean narrative.

An even more explicit example of the structuring of experience by what are perceived as inherited obligations occurs in another story which ties together events at several generations' remove from one another and separated by the whole expanse of the eastern Mediterranean. As a coda to his account of Dareius' invasion of Scythia, Herodotus attaches events which occurred 'at the same time', and which led to an Egyptian involvement in power struggles between Greeks and native tribes at Cyrene in Libya. By way of introduction, his story starts several generations earlier (4.145.1): 'The descendants in the male line ['sons of sons'] of the crew of the *Argo* were expelled from Lemnos by the Pelasgians who had kidnapped the Athenian women from Brauron.' (This last event is one that as yet Herodotus has not even alluded to: he actually tells the story only two books later, at 6.137–9!). These descendants of the crew of the *Argo* sail to Sparta and set up camp and light fires on Mount Taygetos; the Spartans send envoys to discover who they are and where they come from. The new arrivals reply that they are Minyans who have 'returned to their ancestors'; they ask for their share of the rights of citizens and some part of the land. The request is granted, specifically because the 'sons of Tyndareus', Castor and Polydeuces, who were from Sparta, had been on the voyage of the *Argo*. Tensions arise at Sparta and these 'Minyans' are later sent as colonists to the island of Thera, where they settle alongside 'the kinsmen' of the leader of the expedition, whose maternal ancestry at four generations remove is traced back to the Phoenicians who founded Thebes, and who also colonized Thera 'eight generations' before the arrival of the new colonists (4.145–8). A close parallel to this kind of pervasive sense of a web of kinship obligations underlying experience comes again from the Nuer, where tensions between subsections of a Nuer tribe and the granting of asylum by one subsection to members of another

are traced to such inherited obligations: 'the Leng replied
... that they could not refuse asylum to their sisters' sons'.[6]

Thus obligations provide the underlying rationale of Herodotean narrative. But we should remind ourselves that the
choice of narrative as the form in which Herodotus presents
the results of his enquiries was not itself forced upon him.
To record the past and to rescue the experience of men from
the threat of oblivion, as Herodotus undertakes to do in his
opening sentence, is not the same thing as to tell a story.
The fear that what men have lived through and have done,
even the fact that they have lived at all, may vanish into noth-
ingness with the passage of time is perhaps one which all
men have felt, and have tried in different ways (by the building
of tombs in stone or in mounds of earth, or by memorizing
genealogies and transmitting the memory from one generation
to the next) somehow to prevent. But the use of story to
memorialize the past is not universal, and Herodotus' decision
to tell a story is not a simple consequence of his other decision,
to record.

We can form some idea of one sort of record that Herodotus
might have made, instead of telling a story, if we look at
an example of an annalistic table, a chronicle or calendar
of the past, such as the annals kept by monks at Sant Gall
of events in the eighth century. The table gives us a sequence
of years and of events, but some years are empty, without
event; there is no discernible subject, either in the sense of
a central 'character' in the sequence of events nor in the sense
of a guiding 'theme' to which the events recorded may be
supposed to relate. They seem to belong to no single category
of happening or action and they exhibit no principle of connection; it is a sequence without beginning, middle or end,
above all without narrative expectation, that is to say without
any sense of movement towards a closure which, when
reached, will seem to have been implicit in the whole shape
of the story from its beginning, so that we have the essential
of a true story, the sense of an ending. With catalogues of
this kind in the form of genealogies Herodotus was certainly
familiar, as we have seen, though evidence for the existence
of annalistic records in the stricter sense is lacking.[7]

Of another form of contemporary 'historical' record Herodotus shows perhaps some knowledge.[8] That is the royal inscriptions of kings, such as the Assyrian kings or the Persian Kings Dareius and Xerxes. Herodotus describes an inscription in Greek and Persian (4.87) set up by Dareius to commemorate the building of his bridge over the Bosphorus in preparation for the invasion of Scythia, and another inscription commemorating Dareius' visit to the source of the river Tearos (4.91); his knowledge that Dareius completed the canal from the Nile to the Bitter Lakes begun by the pharaoh Necho (2.158.1) may also be due to his having seen Dareius' bilingual inscription recording his achievements. It is possible, since his account of Dareius' accession to power is strikingly similar to the account given on the inscription, that he knew of a version of the great inscription that Dareius set up on the rock face at Behistun recording the events. But it is perhaps more likely, as we have seen, that Herodotus' knowledge of these things derives from a Greek in the service of the Persian king or from the oral tradition of the family of Dareius' fellow conspirator, Megabyxos. But whatever Herodotus may have known of records of this sort, it is certain that his own record of past events owes nothing at all in form or spirit to them. They exist to declare to the world, in standardized and formulaic language, the effortless achievements and absolute righteousness of the king and the unending favour of the god under whose protection he achieved his victories. Of defeats, setbacks, compromises and failures they know nothing; their motivations are stereotyped and they show no trace at all of any narrative interest.

Given his choice of a narrative form for his record of the past, the only model available to Herodotus for storytelling on the scale to which he had committed himself was the epic tradition of narrative that reached back to Homeric epic, to the *Iliad* and the *Odyssey*, and was still very much a living form in Herodotus' own day. Indeed in the work of his cousin Panyassis later writers saw it as having had something of a revival. Very little of Panyassis' work survives, but from the few seemingly rather miserable fragments and from external evidence we can see at least that narrative expansiveness was still (or perhaps once more) the hallmark of epic poetry. In particular it is clear that Panyassis had inherited from Homeric epic the use of long speeches to bring variation of pace and weight and to give perspective to the narrative.

Herodotus declares his indebtedness to epic narrative tradition and his own role as continuator of that tradition by the use of the Greek word meaning 'without renown' in his opening statement of intent: 'and so that great and astonishing achievements, displayed by both Greeks and non-Greeks, may not be without renown'. 'Renown', the *klea andron* ('renown of men'), is the declared subject of epic poetry.[9]

As an example of Herodotean narrative on the larger scale which may illustrate the variety of its forms, its use of speeches and above all the way in which a continuous fabric of story is woven out of a mass of local traditions, I will take the account that Herodotus gives of the tyrants of Corinth, Cypselos and Periander. Neither of these men plays a direct part in the story of conflict between Greeks and Persians, nor does Herodotus offer a continuous narrative of the Corinthian tyranny, but at three points in the larger narrative local traditions about these men are woven into the fabric of Herodotus' story. The first (1.19–24) comes in the form of a local variant on the story that Herodotus is telling of the kings of Lydia before Croesus. Croesus' father, Alyattes, inherits a war against the Ionian Greek city of Miletus from his father Sadyattes; after eleven years of annual fighting, the temple of Athena at Assessos in Milesian territory is accidentally burned down in the course of destroying the Milesians' grain crops. Alyattes falls into a prolonged illness and sends envoys to Apollo at Delphi to seek a cure; they return with a report that the Pythia will not give an answer to their questions until Athena's temple is rebuilt. This tradition Herodotus attributes to the Delphians, but he records in passing a local variant from Miletus that Thrasyboulos, the tyrant of Miletus at the time, was advised how he should act in the light of the oracle (the nature of the advice is not specified) by Periander, tyrant of Corinth, who had close ties of 'ritualized friendship' (*xenia*) with him. Herodotus continues with the story of how Thrasyboulos dissuaded the Lydian king from going on with the war,[10] how he and Alyattes established ties of *xenia*, how Alyattes built two temples, not one, to Athena at Assessos, and how he recovered from his illness. The story is complete, but at this point Herodotus adds a Corinthian story of 'the most astonishing thing that happened to Periander in his lifetime'. This is the story of how Arion, the greatest singer of his day, was forced by the crew of a Corinthian ship on which he was sailing back to Corinth from Tarentum in southern Italy to jump overboard far out at sea and swim for his life, leaving on board the great sums of money he was bringing home. Arion is rescued by a dolphin, brought to shore in the southern Peloponnese at Taenarum (where he dedicates a statue of the dolphin with himself on its back), and makes his way to Corinth, where he is later confronted by Periander with the murderous sailors (1.23–4). This story complete, Herodotus resumes his main narrative at once with the death of Alyattes.

The story of Arion has no causal connection with the surrounding narrative (and in this it is exceptional), but it illustrates a narrative device used by Herodotus which has no precedent in epic poetry; that is, the story related entirely in indirect speech ('the Corinthians have a story that ...'). The whole inserted narrative (something over a page of printed Greek) is told in this form, which in Greek does not require, as it does in English, any repetition of the leading verb 'they say that ...', but is distinguished from the surrounding direct narrative by the forms of the verbs within the story itself. This fact, and the brevity of the story as well as the complete absence of speeches within it, marks the story of Arion both as a subordinate insertion into the main narrative and as a story told entirely on the authority of others than the storyteller. The technique of narrative in indirect speech is one that Herodotus uses on a number of occasions to distance himself as storyteller from a particular section of his narrative: it is used, for example, in the first book to recount the whole tradition of legendary rape and counter-rape (covering two pages of Greek) with which his work opens (1.1–4), a tradition which he explicitly sets aside in order to begin again with what he himself sees as the true starting-point of his narrative, namely the story of Croesus, which is told in direct form; it is used to recount long sections (as we have seen) of what seems to be the special case of Croesus on the pyre (1.86.3–4; 86.5; 87.3); and used again to recount the story of the great Lydian famine which caused the Lydians to send half their population overseas to Italy (1.94.3–7), as well as for incidental stories such as the tale of the advice of Bias (or perhaps Pittakos: Herodotus' sources were divided) to Croesus (1.27), and the tale of how Thales diverted the River Halys to enable Croesus' army to cross (1.75.4–5): the last of these Herodotus again explicitly rejects as incredible.

Periander now disappears from Herodotus' narrative for more than two books and reappears in the wholly different and unconnected context of Spartan intervention in the affairs of Samos (3.44–53). The Spartans had been asked to intervene by Samian exiles, opponents of Polycrates, and the episode is introduced as a sort of coda to the story of Polycrates, Amasis and the ring, by the words: 'It was against Polycrates at the height of his success in everything that the Spartans sent an expedition on the invitation of the Samians who afterwards founded Cydonia in Crete.' The purely temporal connection recalls the story of Arion, but the invitation is then explained by the story of an unsuccessful attempt by Polycrates to get rid of his opponents by sending them in a fleet of forty triremes to help Cambyses in his invasion of Egypt; the Spartan acceptance of the invitation is accounted for by two conflicting stories, one of obligation, the other of revenge. The first is a Samian story of an earlier action on their part to assist Sparta in her struggles with the Messenians and consequent Spartan gratitude; the other a Spartan story of Samian villainy in stealing the great *krater* they had sent to Croesus and a magnificent tunic of fine linen embroidered with gold thread which Amasis had intended as a gift to them. Herodotus then adds that the Corinthians also took part in this expedition against Samos because of an insult offered them by the Samians in the previous generation. This episode involves a story of how Periander had sent three hundred of the sons of the leading families of Corcyra to be made eunuchs at the court of Alyattes, king of Lydia, who had then been rescued from their intended fate and returned to Corcyra by the Samians. This in turn introduces a further story to explain Periander's desire for revenge on the Corcyreans, a story which Herodotus now tells even though he acknowledges that Periander was already dead at the time of the expedition against Samos. Throughout it is the twin notions of obligation and revenge that generate the narrative.

The pace of the narrative slows and becomes more expansive as Herodotus tells the story of the feud between Periander and his younger son, Lycophron, a story involving much more surface detail, precisely focused, and a considerable and beautifully calculated use of direct speech so as to create utterly compelling, startlingly 'modern' portraits of both father and son. Periander has killed his own wife (his motive is never explained) and their younger son, prompted by a hint from his maternal grandfather, breaks off all communication with him and is in turn cut off from even the most minimal human contact by his father's proclamation to the Corinthians making him 'untouchable'. However, coming upon his son, filthy and starving, huddled in an arcade, Periander is moved to pity and tries to remake the relationship, only to be rejected in his turn by his son, whom he then exiles to Corcyra. Later, as he grows old and feels the need of a successor, Periander tries once more to persuade Lycophron to return home and become tyrant of Corinth in his place: his messenger returns without even the favour of an answer. As an argument that cannot fail, Periander next sends his daughter, Lycophron's sister, to Corcyra with a carefully structured speech of persuasive appeal learned from her father: this time Lycophron's reply is that he will never return to Corinth until he hears news of his father's death. Periander makes one last move and suggests that he himself go to Corcyra while Lycophron comes to Corinth and succeeds him, so that they exchange places without the danger of their meeting. To this Lycophron agrees, but just as he sets out for Corinth, with his father ready to make the journey to Corcyra, the Corcyreans make their first appearance as agents in the story and Lycophron is killed to prevent the hated Periander from coming to their island. The story is one of non-communication, in which the words of Lycophron's grandfather, of his sister and of Periander himself are given to us directly, in pointed contrast to the 'silence' of Lycophron who never speaks and whose words appear only in indirect form. The powerful feelings which dictate the behaviour of father and son are nowhere directly acknowledged in Herodotus' text but exist for the reader only through the structuring of the narrative. By contrast with a whole range of other Herodotean stories an overwhelming bitterness between humans so closely tied holds back from violence except in the 'framing' actions of Periander's killing of his wife and the Corcyreans' murder of his son; these lie half outside the story and, as the Corcyreans themselves are outsiders to the feud, their incursion into the last sentence of the tale, with a motive equally unseen until this moment, is stunning in its effect.

The story has a scale and a power and weight out of all proportion to its overt function as an explanatory link in the larger narrative, and in this it resembles a whole range of other Herodotean stories. One that we may compare with it is the story of Adrastus and Atys, embedded in the larger narrative of Croesus in the first book (1.34–45). The story of Adrastus is a story of tragic coincidence; it too is introduced by a temporal connection ('after Solon had gone away'). Adrastus, a prince of the Phrygian royal house, comes as a suppliant to Croesus' court, asking to be ritually purified of the pollution of having accidentally killed his own brother. He is received by Croesus as a friend through his ancestry and lives with the king in his palace. Croesus has had a dream that his own son Atys will be killed by an iron spear, and when an appeal comes to him from a distant part of his kingdom to send dogs and hunters in his son's charge to rid the countryside of a huge and savage boar, he at first refuses the request to send his son. The son, however, convinces him that the boar cannot be the threat that the dream foretold, and so Croesus allows him to go, in the safekeeping of Adrastus, whose own wishes to the contrary are overcome by his obligation to Croesus. The hunting party succeeds in surrounding the boar and moves in for the kill: a spear thrown by Adrastus strikes the son of Croesus and kills him. When the body arrives back at Sardis, with Adrastus following the corpse, he offers his life as owed to Croesus and as unliveable after the double disaster that has befallen him. Croesus refuses to accept the offer, though he accepts Adrastus' sentence of death upon himself as just. Adrastus waits for silence and, standing upon the tomb-mound, cuts his own throat.

Here again the power of the story, which has the effect of almost detaching it from its narrative context, resides in the control of pace and in the masterly interweaving of direct and indirect speech. Most of the interchanges within the story, a full dozen of them, are presented as direct speech, but at two crucial moments Herodotus distances us from the narrative by the language of indirect speech. The first is in Croesus' bitter and horrified outcry to Zeus on hearing of his son's death (1.44.2): to Zeus as protector of the ties of hospitality, as protector of the hearth and as protector of the ties of comradeship, in all three of which relations Croesus feels himself to have been terribly betrayed. The second is in Adrastus' verdict upon himself, delivered as he stands before the body of Croesus' son and holds out his hands in token of submission to Croesus (1.45.1). The control of pace and weight is most palpable in the final sentence, where all the tensions of the story are gathered together to be released in the last terrible clause: 'Adrastus, the son of Gordias, grandson of Midas, he who found himself his own brother's murderer, and murderer of the man who had purified him, when silence fell upon the men around the tomb, recognizing himself to be the most ill-fated of all men he knew, cut his own throat upon the mound.' Adrastus' ancestry and his life-history are gathered in to define him in the moment of his death with an effect that is reminiscent of the 'obituaries' of dead warriors in the *Iliad*, and 'the most ill-fated', in Greek one word of seven syllables, falls with the weight of an axe-blow across the culmination of the story.[11]

What we see, then, in Herodotean narrative is the use of obligation, whether in the form of gratitude or revenge, as the generative principle by which one story evokes another. But the narrative impulse itself constantly generates stories of such scale and weight that they tend to float free and to be read as almost independent of their connection with the overall narrative, the history of developing conflict between Greeks and Persians. It is this impulse towards expansiveness, the tendency to generate stories on a large scale, that provokes in the reader who looks beyond the immediate narrative context, with its lucidity and smooth onward flow, the question, How did I get here? The answer, with very few exceptions, is through a chain of (often inherited) obligations.

The stories that result have often a further secondary function within the surrounding narrative of Greek–Persian conflict. They provide focal points of personal emotion within a narrative that in its all-inclusive sweep involves whole cities, tribes and peoples, with armies that Herodotus numbers as running into millions, in conflict on a huge geographical scale. The technique has analogies with that of Tolstoy in *War and Peace*.

Yet another aspect of storytelling is illustrated for us by the last appearance of Periander within the larger narrative (5.91–3). At a date which Herodotus gives as around 500 BC the Spartans come to regret their earlier action in expelling Hippias, the Peisistratid tyrant, from Athens and allowing the establishment of democracy. They call an assembly of delegates from their allies, in the hope that a joint decision can be taken to restore Hippias to power with the backing of a Peloponnesian expeditionary force. The Spartan proposal is briefly made and supported by arguments of self-interest and the need to make good a breach of the obligations of *xenia* between the Peisistratids and the royal house of Sparta. It is openly opposed only by the delegate from Corinth, Sosikles, who makes a long speech of almost five pages of printed Greek arguing firstly, that it is inconsistent of the Spartans to impose tyranny on another city when they themselves have been uniquely successful in avoiding it in their own community, and secondly, that tyranny is the most evil and vicious form of government known to man. He supports this second argument by a long narrative of Corinthian experience of tyranny. This begins with the birth-story of Kypselus (see p. 41 above) and goes on with the tale of the Milesian tyrant Thrasyboulos' advice to Kypselus' son, Periander: this

55

advice mirrors the advice of Periander to Thrasyboulos which we have already encountered in the first appearance of Periander in Herodotus' narrative (p. 49 above). The story is the famous one of the messenger taken on a walk through a field of standing wheat, during which Thrasyboulos, saying nothing in reply to Periander's enquiry about how he should best control his city, knocks off the heads of any wheat-ears that had risen above the rest. Periander took the point of the message and from then on killed, exiled and confiscated the property of all the leading citizens of Corinth. The culminating instance of Periander's viciousness involves another story: the story of how, prompted by an apparition of his dead wife at an oracle of the dead, Periander summoned the women of Corinth to the temple of Hera, had them all stripped naked, and as an offering to his wife burned their clothing, which had been elaborate and sumptuous to suit what the women had taken to be a festival honouring the goddess. 'Such is tyranny, and such are its deeds,' ends Sosikles, telling of this story, and his argument is closed by a terse warning that Corinth will not support the attempt to restore Hippias. In Sosikles' story there is no direct speech, though the story is told in direct, not indirect, form and though Sosikles quotes verbatim three oracles given by the Pythia to the family of Periander and to the Corinthians. But the technique of telling a story at great length and leisurely pace within a persuasive speech has an epic precedent in the story of Meleager told by Phoinix in the ninth book of the *Iliad* (*Iliad* 9.434–605: the Meleager story itself runs from 527 to 599 and also involves no direct speech), when the envoys from the Greek fleet try to persuade Achilles to return to the fighting. The difference from the *Iliad* is, of course, equally striking: instead of a story told persuasively by one individual hero to another in a small group of men sitting together in a hut, Herodotus records a tradition of storytelling (he does not give his source) in the context of open debate among the delegates of Sparta's Peloponnesian alliance. I have already suggested that such use of narrative as persuasion, with its overtones of heroic poetry, would have been unimaginable in such a political context only a generation later.

In another way too Sosikles' speech, and the stories of Periander and Kypselos in particular, present analogies with Homeric epic while remaining precisely and essentially Herodotean. The language of Herodotus is strikingly non-figurative: phrases such as 'Sparta shot up and flourished' (1.66) or 'Egypt is the gift of the Nile' (2.5.1) are exceptional; by and large he does not use metaphor or simile, even of the formulaic 'with hair as black as a raven' type, but above all never extended simile of the familiar Homeric form.[12] These presumably had no place in the oral traditions on which Herodotus is drawing. When Herodotus says that one thing is like another, the comparison, to whatever length it may be drawn, rests on a quite literal level of resemblance. Figurative speech is replaced by the description of figurative action or is reserved for the language of oracles, and that pairing is no coincidence. There are good examples of what I have called figurative action not only in the story of Thrasyboulos' advice to Periander but also in the gift by the Scythian tribes to Dareius of a bird, a mouse, a frog and five arrowheads,[13] in the Aethiopian king's present of a longbow to Cambyses and in the Cypriot king Euethon's gift of a golden spindle and distaff to Pheretime of Cyrene (4.131–2; 3.21–2; 4.162). In all these cases the action of present-giving is to be read as a figurative statement of limitation, of the recipient's inability to match and overcome the giver, or as a warning to stay within the limits of a sexual role. In the case of the Scythian gift the parallel with the figurative language of oracles is made strikingly clear; but for simile in the accepted sense Herodotus has no use. Nonetheless another function of the Homeric simile is taken over by the parenthetical tale within Herodotus' narrative: both serve to open up the world of the narrative, more narrowly conceived and defined, to admit relevant but different areas of human experience. In a sense, Herodotus' narrative takes in the whole history of the Greeks and their neighbours to the east and south in the several generations from the mid-sixth century until the second decade of the fifth. It does so not by having that history as its overt and acknowledged subject, but by systematically gathering in local traditions from all over the Greek-speaking world and enclosing them in the looping and eddying course of the overall narrative of conflict between Greeks and barbarians, in what Herodotus himself seems to have thought of simply as 'additions'. In the middle of discussing the cold of the Scythian winter and the inability of mules and donkeys to survive in the climate of Scythia (4.28–30), Herodotus suddenly remarks: 'I am actually surprised (my story has looked for additions from the outset) that in the whole territory of Elis mules cannot be born, though the area is not cold and there is no other evident cause.' The absence of mules in Elis, in the Peloponnese of mainland Greece, opens up our understanding of Scythian geography in much the same parenthetical (or, in Herodotean terms, 'additional') way that the stories of Arion and Periander enlarge and fill out our sense of the experience of men. And it is very revealing of Herodotus' cast of mind that the phrase 'I am surprised' or the adjective 'astonishing' should so often introduce a parenthesis: as Momigliano has remarked, Herodotus is the paradigm of the historian whom everything 'astonishes'.[14]

The comparison with a river implicit in describing Herodotean narrative as 'looping and eddying' would probably not have surprised his original audience. Two centuries after Herodotus, the poet Callimachus could compare Homeric epic with the River Euphrates, a great river full of water but the water itself clouded with mud and silt: it is not a bad comparison (if we make allowances for Callimachus' preference for a rivulet of clear water) and Herodotus might well have accepted it for his own work. He himself describes how the course of the Euphrates above Babylon loops so much that one passes the same village three times on successive days: reading his narrative one knows what he means (1.185).

I will end this chapter with a consideration of the relationship between narrative and theory in Herodotus. When the reader reaches the end of the story, in the summer of 479 BC, he finds Herodotus closing the whole with a last tale: one that we seem, in part, to have heard before (9.119–22). Herodotus has just recorded the last event of the last year of his narrative: it is the crucifixion of the cruel and clever Artayktes, Persian governor of the Gallipoli peninsula, outside Sestos, at the precise spot where Xerxes had brought ashore his bridge across the Hellespont (another echo, this time of the revenge of Kandaules' wife in the first book, 'launched from the very place where he showed me naked': 1.11.5). He goes on to record a story of the great-grandfather of Artayktes, Artembares. This man had suggested to the Persians that they abandon their own small and rugged country and seize possession of some other, better land, so that they might control all of Asia. Cyrus replies that 'soft country makes soft men': 'if they should do what Artembares suggested, they must prepare themselves not to rule but to be ruled. Good fighters and good food are not the product of the same soil.' The theme of the relationship between luxuriance and power echoes back through the whole story. Before Croesus attacked the Persians, he had been advised against the plan by Sandanis (1.71): if it succeeded, it would be to conquer a land of men who wore leather because they had no other fabric, who ate only what they had, not what they wanted 'since their country was rugged', men without figs, without wine, without any other good thing. If it failed, these men would have tasted good things and would cling to them. Thank God, that he had never put it into *their* minds to attack the Lydians. Croesus was not persuaded. The theme recurs in Cyrus' figurative but concrete presentation of a choice of lives to the Persian tribesmen (1.125.2–126): a day of clearing the hillside of thorny scrub with sickles is followed by a day of feasting and drinking in a meadow. The Persians choose the good things, and Cyrus promises them freedom and the power to match the Medes in war as well (the story is hardly consistent with the story of Cyrus and Artembares that closes Herodotus' history: they correspond like a pair of complementary proverbs). A little later in the first book, the Lydians rebel from their newly established Persian overlords and Cyrus asks Croesus for his advice: should he enslave them, since as things are it is as if he has killed the father but spared the children (1.155–157.2). Croesus' advice is to remove any further threat from the Lydians by making them reverse their way of life: they must be made to abandon arms, and take up soft clothing and soft shoes, teach their children to play the harp and to buy and sell; so they will soon become women where they were once men. Finally, a pair of contrasting episodes: first Mardonius, presenting the case to Xerxes for a Persian invasion of Greece, suggests that Europe is a paradise, with cultivated trees of every kind and soil pre-eminent in its quality, fit only for a king of Persia to possess, and inhabited by men feeble in fighting and ripe for conquest by the Persians, 'best of all men in warfare' (7.5.3; 7.9.2a–c); second, the Spartan Demaratus tells Xerxes that Greece has learned the capacity to resist any attempt to enslave her by having always had 'poverty as her foster-sister' (7.102). The idea which in these episodes threads its way through Herodotus' narrative is the issue of the relationship between hardship and toughness on the one hand and ease and softness on the other; repeatedly it is related to environment as well as to culture, as it is again in Herodotus' account of the Ionian Greeks whose climate is 'the most perfect of all men we know', but who are 'the weakest of all Greek peoples and of least account', ashamed of the very name of Ionians (1.142.1–2; 143.2–3). Herodotus' narrative does not 'solve' the problem at issue (narrative thinking is not that kind of thing) but it presents it, through recurring and balancing narrative episodes, for his audience to weigh for themselves.[15]

So too with the most prominent of all the threads of Herodotus' fabric of narrative, the thread of war. War and conflict between Greeks and non-Greeks is Herodotus' declared subject from the start; it is another aspect of his inheritance from heroic epic, and it is in turn a major part of his own legacy to European historiography, from Thucydides right through to the present. But Herodotus' attitude to war, like that of Homer, is profoundly ambiguous. For both, one has the feeling that the centrality of war as a subject for narrative is not merely due to the central place of warfare in the everyday world of the writer and his audience, but also to its figurative importance within the ancient Greek perception of man and his experience. Heraclitus' words, 'war is the father of all things' (fr. 53 DK), are not merely the first limb of a Heraclitean paradox but a metaphorical statement of a central truth of human life: life is structured by the principle of reciprocating

exchange and one aspect of that principle is conflict. Of conflict war is the ultimate expression and at the same time the
ultimate theatre for the 'display' of 'great and astonishing
achievements', a theatre where success and failure are visible
to all and awesome in their consequences, and which, in
Homeric epic, numbers even the gods among its audience.
In the *Iliad* war occupies only the foreground of a depiction
of human life as a whole, and for Herodotus also the 'astonishing achievements' of warfare are not to be distinguished from
other achievements, such as driving a tunnel through a mountain to bring water to a waterless city or making a marvellous
tunic out of fine linen and gold thread. But warfare is different
in kind in that it evokes contrary responses, one would guess,
both in Herodotus and in his audience. Croesus is asked by
Cyrus (1.87.3–4) what man persuaded him to attack his
country, and Croesus rejects the implication that such advice
could have come from a man at all: it was not a man but
a god, the 'god of the Greeks', 'for no one is so mindless
that he chooses war instead of peace: in peace it is sons who
bury their fathers, in war fathers bury their sons.' It must
have been a god: the inhuman senselessness, the unnaturalness of war are perfectly expressed. The thought is echoed
in the mention of twenty ships that Athens sent to aid the
Ionian revolt, 'the beginning of miseries for both Greeks and
barbarians', and again when the Athenians withdraw their
claim to command the Greek fleet at Artemisium in the face
of a refusal by their allies to fight under them (8.2.2–3.1).
Herodotus, in his own voice, it seems, approves their
decision: 'for violent conflict within one people is a thing
as much worse than war fought by united allies, as war is
worse than peace'. Yet no one, reading Herodotus' narrative,
could suppose that this verdict was for him a simple truth:
the story presents a more complex reality than the proverbial
generalization which the Greeks called a *gnome*, and unlike
the *gnome* it perhaps sets its target as presenting the totality
of the real, so that judgment is once more left to the audience
and not enforced by the simple assertion of a general 'truth'.
A measure of that complexity is given by Herodotus' accounts
of heroic action and death in battle. The Greek for 'he died

a heroic death' means literally 'he became the best of men and died'. It is possible, as in the case of Cleobis and Biton (1.31.4–5), to 'become the best of men' other than by dying on the battlefield, but that is exceptional. Death in war remains the characteristic and defining context in which that phrase is used: it is the verdict passed in unqualified and simple admiration on Leonidas at Thermopylae (7.224.1) and on others who died in that battle (7.226.1–2), notably Deioces the Spartan who, when told by a local Greek that when the Persian army fired its bows the sunlight was cut off by the mass of arrows, replied that it would be good to fight in the shade. Herodotus' attitude to those who died at Thermopylae is uncomplicated. The dead of Plataea evoke a more complex response (9.71.2–4): the Spartan Aristodemus, Herodotus asserts as his own opinion, died the most heroic death and became 'by far the best', but his fellow Spartans who were present at the battle demur, since Aristodemus sought his own death, 'doing heroic things after leaving the ranks in a frenzy of madness', in order to blot out the shame of being the only survivor of Thermopylae; Poseidonios was 'the better man' because he did not want to die. The extreme case of a divided judgment is the case of Pytheas, a soldier on the deck of one of the first Greek ships to be taken by the Persians in the opening skirmishes of the invasion (7.181.1–2): Pytheas fights on when his ship is taken and 'becomes the best of men'. He fights 'until he was completely butchered' – the Greek word implies, even more unambiguously than the English, a comparison with the butchery of meat; there is a shock of revulsion to be registered, even in the pronouncement of admiration for the man's heroism.

It is easy to suppose, mistakenly I think, that Herodotus, just because he is a 'maker of stories', as he would have been the first to agree, is not a thinker and presents no argument. In fact, his greatness as a storyteller lies in the thinking as well as the feeling that his story requires of us, his audience, as an adequate response to his own complexities: the balance of admiration and distress that his narrative reveals is the product of, as well as the stimulus to, profound and complex thinking.

4 Why Things Happen

In this chapter I want to consider Herodotus' perception of why things happen and to argue against two prevalent views of him which seem at first sight to stem from diametrically opposed interpretations of his purpose. One of these views attributes to Herodotus an inherently trivial use of causal connections, the other an intensely serious 'philosophy of history', but I shall argue that both stem from the inability to take Herodotus seriously on his own terms, as a storyteller whose view of the world and whose modes of explanation are rooted both in the traditions of his craft and in the cultural assumptions common to storyteller and audience.

Herodotus' first sentence involves him in a commitment not merely to record the past but also to explain it, to give 'the cause which set Greeks and non-Greeks at war with one another'. But Mabel Lang, for example, in her recent book *Herodotean Narrative and Discourse*, speaks of 'Herodotus' concern with a kind of personal motivation that is useful from a narrative point of view *rather than* with historical causes', and elsewhere of 'narrative convenience' specifically as contrasted with 'historical causes'.[1] This reading of Herodotus, which essentially dismisses his treatment of historical causation, seems to go back to an article published in 1971 by Jacqueline de Romilly, on vengeance as a form of historical explanation in Herodotus.[2] There Mme de Romilly makes a similar distinction between the idea of revenge as 'a convenient form of linkage' ('une liaison commode') – convenient, that is, for the storyteller – on the one hand, and on the other 'serious analysis'; Herodotus, she suggests, adopts revenge as an explanation for human behaviour because it gives him 'a system of linear connection which is superficial, even artificial, but which allows him to sew together a greater number of anecdotes or descriptions'. To suppose that this is all that revenge means for Herodotus is to misread him in a quite fundamental way. We have seen, in the previous chapter, how the obligation of revenge forms an important strand of narrative connection in Herodotus and constitutes one aspect of the impulse to generate narrative: in this chapter we have to see the narrative connection as simultaneously a framework of explanation.

The storyteller characteristically asks 'how did it all begin?': so in his opening chapters Herodotus records that it 'all began', according to the Persians, with the abduction of Io by the Phoenicians – this action 'began the wrongdoing'. The abduction of Europa restores the balance (it is tit for tat, 'equals for equals' in Herodotus' expressive phrase) and that of Medea marks a new beginning, this time by the Greeks, to which Helen's abduction is in turn a reply. The Trojan War is yet another new beginning: 'they began a military expedition against Asia, before ever the Persians invaded Europe'. The opening chapters recall the opening of the *Iliad*: 'Which of the gods set the two to fight in conflict? It was Zeus' son and Leto's. For he was angry with the king... because the son of Atreus had insulted Chryses his priest. For Chryses had come....' The storyteller backtracks to a 'beginning'; the story is under way, and with it the explanation of 'Achilles' wrath'.

Of course, as Mme de Romilly stresses, Herodotus rejects this series of legendary abductions as the real, serious starting-point of his story: it was Croesus whom he 'knows' as 'first beginning the wrongdoing' (1.5.3). But Herodotus rejects the abductions *not* because revenge is not a serious explanation, but because he cannot say 'whether these things happened as I have narrated them or in some other way'; it is the facts, not the explanation, that he cannot take seriously. And one thing we should not doubt is the seriousness of Herodotus' commitment to explain.

The whole texture of Herodotus' writing is soaked in the explanatory mode: the narrative connection is constantly made through inferential particles ('for', 'therefore', 'and so' rather than 'then', 'next'), and significantly, since it is another aspect of the narrative mode of explanation, the backward-looking connection is much commoner than the forward. 'For' is more than three times as common a connective in Herodotus as 'and so' or 'therefore' (479 instances, as against 136 of 'therefore'). That is to say, the assertion of fact is made, and the narrator looks back to some previous event or outward to some general truth in order to explain. 'He did this', 'he said this, for . . .'.

The nature of the explanatory connection is not simple or stereotyped; Herodotus' understanding of why things happen is complex and subtle. It covers notions of responsibility and perhaps of guilt; it embraces contributory factors as well as cause. On the larger scale, the framework of explanation, as we shall see, is structured by the underlying assumption of reciprocity – the all-embracing assumption, that is, that all human action, for good or ill, will be balanced by counteraction in the same mode. The obligations of gratitude and revenge are the fundamental human motives for Herodotus just as, as we have already seen, they are the primary stimulus to the generation of narrative itself. The chain of obligation and revenge leads back from Salamis, Plataea and Marathon to Croesus and thence to Gyges or to the rape of Io. But within this larger frame of reference, Herodotus' perception of causation embraces variety and multiplicity in the answers that he gives to the question: why did this happen?

Let me take as an example the beginning of Book Three (3.1–9): Cambyses, son of Cyrus the Great, succeeds to the throne of Persia and begins a campaign against the Egyptian Pharaoh, Amasis, 'for the following reason' (*aitie*). The explanation lies in a story within a story: Cambyses had asked to marry a daughter of Amasis, on the suggestion of an Egyptian doctor at the Persian court, who wanted his own revenge on the Pharaoh for having separated him from his wife and children and having sent him to Persia at the request of Cambyses' father, who had asked Amasis for the best eye-doctor in Egypt. Cambyses' request for the marriage was intended by the Egyptian doctor either to cause Amasis distress, by separating him from his daughter, if he agreed, or to make him Cambyses' enemy if he refused. Amasis felt unable to do either: he was afraid of Persian power but he knew that Cambyses would humiliate him by treating the girl as his concubine and not as his wife. He solved the dilemma by sending to Persia the tall and beautiful daughter of his predecessor as pharaoh, Apries, whom he had deposed, and pretending that she was his own daughter. But the girl gave away Amasis' secret and Cambyses, seeing himself in turn insulted, determined on revenge. That, Herodotus says, is the story told in Persia. In Egypt the story is different: it was Cyrus, not Cambyses, who married the daughter of Apries, and Cambyses was her son. That story Herodotus rejects on the grounds that it conflicts with other known facts as well as with well-established Persian custom. But he tells another story, which depends on the same chronology and which he also disbelieves, that would make Cambyses' attack on Egypt the fulfilment of a promise made to his Persian mother when he was ten, a promise that he would 'turn Egypt upside down' for her, to avenge the insult given her by Cyrus in preferring the Egyptian princess to her. Either way the motive is revenge, but in any case, Herodotus adds, there was a contributory factor which helped to bring about the expedition: another story follows. A Halicarnassian mercenary officer in Amasis' service by the name of Phanes, feeling himself ill treated by the Egyptian king, deserted to Cambyses, revealed the details of Amasis' army and above all offered Cambyses a way in which he could get his own army safely across the Sinai desert and thus carry out the invasion he was already planning. The interaction of a variety of personal motives explains why Cambyses embarked on the invasion of Egypt. Elsewhere Herodotus implies other motives also: Amasis had been an ally of Croesus and Cyrus had already before his death had it in mind to attack Egypt, as well as Babylon, the Bactrian tribes and the Saccae (1.77; 1.153–4).

The personal nature of the explanations that Herodotus' storytelling implies is a recurring feature: Persian involvement in the affairs of Samos and the Persian invasion of the island is traced back to Dareius' acknowledgment of obligation to the exiled brother of the Samian tyrant Polycrates, Syloson, who had once, before Dareius became king, given him a magnificent red cloak which Dareius has seen Syloson wearing at Memphis in Egypt when Dareius was Cambyses' spear-bearer and had set his heart on (3.139ff.). The Ionian revolt is in large part explained by Herodotus as the result of the personal power-struggles and complex vendettas of the tyrants who controlled the Ionian cities under Persian protection. Many modern readers of Herodotus have seen this tendency to trace back events to the personal motivations of individuals as a sign of his inability to penetrate below the surface to 'real' or 'underlying' causes of a more abstract and general nature. But on this two things should perhaps be said. One, that here again the likelihood is that Herodotus is giving us the true feel of what men said, of how contemporaries perceived and accounted for the major happenings of their experience. Second, as George Forrest and others have pointed out, that we are hardly in a position to correct Herodotus on such things: his familiarity with the ways and workings of power in a world dominated by ruling families and elites, and by despotic kings surrounded by a closed circle of kinsmen and subordinate officials, is very much greater than our own.[3] Herodotus is not much concerned (by comparison, say, with Ctesias) with the intrigues and gossip of the Persian court except where the major events of his narrative are concerned, but here perhaps we need to give his accounts of how decisions are reached, and on what grounds, more credence than our own cultural assumptions and our confidence in the possession of superior historical insight would always suggest.

A more interesting problem in Herodotus' scheme of explanation, and one that goes to the heart of his perception of historical events, is provided by the supernatural strand of causation that often, in the case of the most momentous happenings, appears alongside and at first sight may seem to override both human motivation and empirically verifiable 'causes'. Croesus' decision to attack the Persian empire, the event from which Herodotus correctly sees confrontation between Greeks and Persians as stemming, is given a quite complex explanation in Herodotus' narrative. On its first introduction Croesus' decision is explained by two factors:

first, his desire to avenge the humiliating deposition of his brother-in-law, the Median king Astyages, by Astyages' daughter's son, Cyrus (1.46.1); and secondly a fear of the growing and expanding power of the Persians under Cyrus and a wish to stop its further growth before it was too late (in our terms, a pre-emptive strike) (1.71.1; 1.73.1). Later, Herodotus elaborates on this first explanation by adding two further motives, on the one hand territorial ambition, and on the other a misplaced trust in the Delphic oracle's reply to his question whether he should take the field against the Persians and in a second oracle which seemed to him to imply that he had nothing to fear from Cyrus. The shadow of the supernatural is already to be seen in these oracles, but after his narrative of Croesus' disastrous military venture Herodotus goes on to tell how Croesus, with Cyrus' permission, sent envoys to Delphi one further time to demand from the god, in insulting terms, an explanation of his apparent hand in Croesus' downfall (1.91). This time ultimate responsibility for the catastrophe that had befallen Croesus is laid on predetermined fate: 'the lot assigned not even a god can escape', begins the oracle's reply, and for Croesus the 'lot assigned' had been to pay for the crime of Gyges, four generations before. Apollo's intervention, the Pythia at Delphi added, though it had not been enough to secure the postponement of disaster for Sardis until the next generation, had gained for Croesus three extra years of prosperity, so that he became the victim of his 'lot' three years later than had been 'assigned' to him. That was the reply brought back to Croesus by his Lydian envoys, according to (Delphic?) tradition, and he accepted it.

The Greek words that I have paraphrased as 'predetermined fate' and translated as 'the lot assigned' (*pepromene moira*) mean literally the 'allotted share'. In a famous passage of the *Iliad* (16.426–61), the notion of an allotted share is discussed by the gods in such as way as to suggest that it is a notion more like the 'rules of the game' than like a natural law or a Calvinistic predetermination. Under the rules there comes a time when a man must die; the rules *could* be ignored or suspended or broken by the gods, but then we would be in a different game and things would not any longer be as we

68

know they are. For Herodotus in the Croesus story the idea seems to be somewhat different, more in the nature of an (almost) irrevocable dispensation made to an individual by a personalized agency: the response of the Pythia refers to 'Fates' (*Moirai*) in the plural, who could not be 'brought round' by Apollo.

The story of Croesus and Cyrus, we have seen, can be shown to rest on traditions that have already been markedly affected by the 'mythologizing' process of oral transmission. It is considerably more disconcerting to find the same intervention of supernatural powers in Xerxes' decision to invade Greece, dated by Herodotus, it seems, to a year or two after the beginning of his reign in 486 BC and thus in all probability less than fifty years before Herodotus wrote his account of how it was reached. Herodotus' understanding of the motives that lay behind Xerxes' decision and the process of debate and argument in the Persian court that preceded it lacks nothing in subtlety, or in sensitivity to the kinds of pressure to which a despot of immense power such as the Persian king might find himself subjected (7.5–20, esp. 5–6, 11.2–4). The account of argument and counter-argument is long and intricate and the resulting picture of a man succumbing to a variety of pressures and interests is not one that we have any *a priori* grounds for rejecting, let alone any positive evidence to set against.[4] The pressures come from powerful families in northern Greece whose power, like that of their counterparts on the Asia Minor seaboard, would be more secure under the protection of the Persian king; from political exiles from Athens (the family of the tyrant Peisistratus) who see their restoration to power as now dependent on Persian backing and who seek revenge on their political opponents for their humiliation, and from ambitious Persians of Xerxes' own immediate entourage who see the conquest of Greece as leading to their own advancement; these pressures are reinforced by tempting oracular predictions produced by a Greek soothsayer planted and backed by the Peisistratids, and above all assisted by a general underestimate of and failure to understand the Greeks on the part both of Mardonius, Xerxes' ambitious first cousin, and of Xerxes himself. They combine with personal motives already present in Xerxes: an obligation, inherited from his father Dareius, to get revenge for Persia on Athens for its support of the Ionian revolt; a desire for some glorious exploit to rank with those of Cyrus, Cambyses and Dareius; and a grandiose wish to make the Persian empire coextensive with the world 'on which the sun shines'. The combination of intrigue, ambition and rhetoric in an atmosphere of fear and flattery has the ring of truth, as does the process of hesitation, of decisions made and unmade, that Herodotus describes.

The shock comes when into this coherent and seemingly complete account of what happened in the king's immediate circle, there is suddenly introduced a supernatural visitation (7.12.1ff.).[5] On the night after the first council meeting, Xerxes dreams that a 'tall and handsome' man speaks to him in his sleep and tells him to return to his decision of the previous day to attack the Greeks; when he does not, the dream returns the following night and threatens him with swift humiliation. In his terror at this second dream, Xerxes insists that his uncle, Dareius' brother Artabanus, who had successfully argued against the expedition, should dress in the royal robes and regalia, sit on the king's throne and sleep in the king's bed, to see whether the dream would visit him also and thus show that it was 'a god' who sent the dream and wished him to invade Greece. Artabanus too has the same dream, which tells him for his part that he will be punished for attempting to 'avert what must be', with the result that Artabanus withdraws his advice, since, it seems, 'destruction driven on them by the gods' is already overtaking the Greeks (7.12–18).

Once more there are things that need to be said about Herodotus' report of Xerxes' decision. The first is that parallel sets of causation, one human, the other supernatural, neither of which renders the other inoperative, are as much a feature of Greek thinking about accountability as they are of their storytelling from Homer onwards, and would not in themselves have proved in any way surprising to Herodotus' original audience. Like another African people who are the subject of a classic of anthropological field-work by Evans-Pritchard, the Azande of the southern Sudan, ancient Greeks accepted what Ieuan Lewis has called a 'luxuriant multiplicity' in their perception of causes.[6] The function of supernatural causation is not, as we might think, to replace or override empirical cause and effect: the Azande are as well aware as anyone else that incompetence in making a pot or a canoe or in building a hut is sufficient cause for the breaking of the pot, the sinking of the canoe or the collapse of the hut. Nor is it the function of a theory of supernatural causation to remove moral responsibility, to make men and women no longer accountable for their actions.[7] In both societies, just as is markedly the case in Herodotus' narrative, supernatural causation is invoked rather to answer a different sort of question: not what causes the downfall of a man from power, or the failure of a man's plan (for these questions empirical answers exist), but why *that* man *then*; why Kandaules, why Xerxes, why *me*, particularly? To quote from Mary Douglas' account of Evans-Pritchard's analysis of Azande notions: 'there is an area of curiosity that they pursue to the depths, though we Westerners leave it unplumbed. That is the ego-focussed question of why any particular mishap should fall on *me* particularly. Why should two causal sequences converge so that I should happen to be in the hunting-party and be in the way when the buffalo turns to gore? Why should I eat bananas every day and today eat one that disagrees with me? Why should the crumbling roof of the granary, bound to collapse one day, collapse on the day when my exposed head is there taking shade? This range of curiosity about the intersection of chains of events with my personal life is met in Azande culture by a set of prepared answers and actions. The most likely explanation is generally witchcraft';[8] or, for ancient Greeks, the envious or vengeful intervention of an angry divinity.[9]

The second thing we might notice is that the story of Xerxes' dream is specifically referred to as 'a story told by Persians' and introduced by a combination of particles which have something of the flavour of 'it seems that': there are perhaps reasons for thinking that Herodotus is not entirely happy with the story of the dream. With this in mind, it is also noticeable that when Herodotus comes to report the reply of the Delphic oracle to Croesus' envoys, he stresses that what he is reporting is 'the story that is told' (this time he does not name his source, though it seems likely enough that it is the Delphians). Here too it may be that he is disclaiming responsibility for the notion of 'what must be' as a factor in the explanation of human experience. But even if that observation is correct, it does not altogether suffice to remove the problem of 'fate' from our attempt to understand Herodotus' sense of why things happen. There are more than a dozen instances else-where in Herodotus' narrative where he invokes phrases like 'disaster had to befall him' or 'what was going to happen', seemingly as explanations of what has occurred; that is, by inserting them into the narrative introduced by particles such as 'for' or conjunctions such as 'since'. And in fully half these cases there is nothing to indicate that the explanation is not Herodotus' own, or at least one accepted by him without misgivings. Even though it is to be observed about explana-tions of this type that there is a *tendency* for them to be invoked in explaining the events of the remoter past, that is to say things that happened in the generations before Dar-eius came to the throne of Persia, it is no more than a tendency. Herodotus invokes 'what had to be' to explain both Demara-tus' deposition as king of Sparta in 491 BC (6.64) and the failure of the Persian expedition of 499 BC to take Naxos (5.33.2); these are unmistakably historical events of no more than ten or fifteen years before his birth, and the explanation is offered by Herodotus in his own person. So we cannot simply say that 'fate' is a notion employed by Herodotus only to explain the distant or legendary past nor that it is simply a mythologiz-ing motif that had by then entered the oral tradition about such events on which Herodotus was drawing.

Does this mean that 'the supreme force in the universe is Fate,' as Geoffrey de Ste Croix has suggested, or, to quote Mabel Lang once more, that Herodotus had an 'apparent historical belief that what is had to be'?[10] In order to answer that question we have to look more closely at the way in which Herodotus employs the idea of what 'had to be'. He does not in fact use very often the notion of 'fate' (*moira*) that the Delphic oracle uses to account for Croesus' downfall, and when he does it is as a passing remark, almost a shrug of the shoulders, twice attributed to characters in his narrative, to dismiss further consideration of why the thing in question happened. Apart from the case of Croesus, he uses the term *moira* on only three occasions: he makes Astyages, for example, say to the boy Cyrus, 'since I did you wrong because of a dream vision that was not fulfilled and you are still alive through your own *moira*...' (1.121); no more needs to be said by way of explanation for Cyrus' survival and the story moves on. So too in reporting the death of Arkesilas of Cyrene, through failure perhaps to understand an oracle, Herodotus in his own person says: 'he fulfilled his *moira*' (that is, he died) 'either as a result of his own deliberate act or because he inadvertently failed to grasp the oracle' (4.164.4): once more, that is Arkesilas' brief and dismissive obituary rather than an explanation of his death and Herodotus proceeds at once to more interesting things. Finally, the Samian tyrant Maiandrios dismisses the question of his predecessor's death by saying to an assembly of the Samians, as a kind of bridge-passage in his account of his own actions, 'well, Polycrates fulfilled his own *moira*' (3.142.3): that is, again, 'he died'. In other words, in these instances the idea of *moira* is not so much an explanation as a means of avoiding the necessity of explanation and the consequent break in the pace and flow of the story. It is certainly no evidence in itself for Herodotus' belief in historical determinism.

The other two notions, the notions of 'what had to be' and 'what was going to happen', occur more frequently, and Herodotus' use of them is more instructive. The phrase 'it had to be' is used on some seven occasions: of Kandaules' suggestion to Gyges that he should see his wife naked ('he said to Gyges (for disaster had to befall Kandaules)...' 1.8.2); of Apries' disastrous decision to attack Cyrene which leads to his own downfall (2.161.3); of the fatal decision by the Scythian king, Skyles, who had already adopted Greek dress, a Greek way of life and Greek religious observances, to be initiated into the mysteries of Dionysus (4.79.1); of the chance that Labda the Corinthian happened to overhear the talk of the men sent to kill her son Cypselus, the future tyrant of Corinth ('disaster for Corinth had to spring from the son of Eetion; for Labda heard all this...': 5.92d.1); of the action of Timo, the priestess of the chthonic gods at Paros, in suggesting to Miltiades that he should enter the holy place of Demeter Thesmophoros on the hill in front of the town, a decision which led to Miltiades' death ('she was not responsible', the Pythia said afterwards, 'because Miltiades had to end badly': 6.134–5, esp. 135.3); and of the miseries that Egypt 'had to' undergo for a hundred and fifty years, and of the failure by Mykerinos, the Egyptian king, to do 'what he had to do', for which he was punished by an early death (2.133.3). A number of things strike the reader about these examples: first, that it is possible, as the last instance shows, not to do what one 'has to do' (though in that case the consequences will perhaps overtake one); second, that in the case of Cypselus, the Corinthian tyrant, the notion of the inevitability of an occurrence is itself presented as an inference from the extraordinary chance that led to his survival; and third, that in the other four cases it is a human decision, not an unmotivated chance event, that is 'explained' by the statement that it 'had to be'. In all of these cases, a momentous or fatal event, which in some sense not easily defined does not 'fit', is given the 'explanation' that it had to happen precisely because no 'ordinary-language' explanation seems to be available. It was not to be expected that Kandaules or Skyles or Arkesilas would do the things they did, and the idea of inevitability substitutes for the missing explanation.

The examples of what 'was going to happen' in Herodotus' narrative suggest another line of thought. In addition to Artabanus' attempt to reverse Xerxes' decision, Herodotus appeals to the idea of inevitability by using this phrase in two other connections: the events that led to the death of Cambyses, and the downfall of Polycrates, tyrant of Samos. In both, the idea of what was 'going to happen' is associated with the idea of discovery, with the realization of a general truth about human experience. Cambyses dreams that his brother Smerdis will kill him and replace him on the Persian throne; he therefore has Smerdis secretly assassinated, only to discover later that two of the priestly caste called Magi, one of them also named Smerdis, had carried out a palace coup and had proclaimed the false Smerdis as the new king of Persia. On hearing of this Cambyses leaps into the saddle of his horse, intending to ride at once back to Susa with his army and put down the usurper. But his leap is fatal: the tip slips from his swordscabbard and he is mortally wounded in the thigh ('in the place where he himself had stabbed the god of the Egyptians, Apis' – both an example of reciprocal action and an uncanny event). Wounded, he asks the name of the place where these things have happened and is told that it is called Ecbatana. Long ago he had received an oracle at Buto in Egypt that he would end his life at Ecbatana, and had supposed that he would die, an old man, at Ecbatana in Media: now it turned out that the oracle had spoken of another Ecbatana, in Syria. At that moment Cambyses 'grasped the oracle' and saw that 'this was the place where it was assigned to him to die'; twenty days later, as he lay dying, he assembled the most notable Persians of his entourage and told them how he had had his brother assassinated, 'for it is not after all in the nature of man to avert what is going to happen'; he had made himself his brother's murderer 'without necessity', because 'I wholly mistook what was going to be' (3.30-2; 61-6, esp. 65.3-4).

The other case of 'what was going to happen' also involves discovery. Herodotus attributes the phrase to the Egyptian pharaoh, Amasis, in a coda to the marvellous story of Polycrates' ring. Amasis had warned Polycrates ('knowing that divinity is envious') that his astonishing record of success and conquest was itself a danger, which only some painful loss could make less threatening. Polycrates throws into the open sea the gold ring set with emeralds that of all things he values most, only to have it brought back to him in the stomach of a magnificent fish presented to him by the fisherman who had caught it. When he reports these events to Amasis, Amasis formally renounces his ties of *xenia* with him: 'he realized then that it is impossible for one man to rescue another from what was going to happen, and that Polycrates, successful in everything, who found even what he threw away, was going to end ill' (3.39.3–43, esp. 43.1).

Both of these are examples of what from Aristotle we have learned to think of as 'tragic discovery' and to associate with fifth-century drama. But in fact the moment of discovery is as old as Achilles' realization in the eighteenth book of the *Iliad* that with the death of Patroclus the granting of his prayer to have Agamemnon and the Greeks humiliated has turned to dust (*Iliad* 18.79ff.).[11] To see that parallel may alert us to a motif deeply embedded in the craft of storytelling and in particular to another Homeric echo, this time precisely in Herodotus' use of the phrase 'what was going to happen'. Time and again in the *Iliad* and the *Odyssey* (forty-eight times in the *Iliad* and thirty-nine in the *Odyssey*) Homer uses phrases such as 'it was going to happen' or 'it was not going to happen', and often they serve precisely to 'point' the narrative, to control the audience's response to his story. After Patroclus' death, Thetis laments to Achilles, her son, that his own death must follow swiftly once he has avenged Patroclus by killing Hector: 'May I die now, at once,' is Achilles' reply, 'since I was not after all to protect my companion as death came on him' (*Iliad* 18.98–9). Homer's 'I was not to' is Herodotus' 'what was going to happen' (both phrases use the Greek verb *mello*), and the sense of discovery and realization is conveyed, as it was in the story of Cambyses, by the Greek particle *ara*, embedded in the phrase and meaning 'so', 'after all', 'as it has turned out'. The moment of realization actualizes the sense of closure, of an ending implicit in the story from its beginning but only now revealed. The same phrase may mark the narrator's foreknowledge of the shape his story is to have: Odysseus comments, as he describes how he and his companions went into the Cyclops' empty cave, 'he was not after all going to be to our liking when he did appear' (*Odyssey* 9.230, again with *ara*). 'He was not going to' may underline the pathos of foreknowledge ('Dolon set off for the ships: he was not after all going to come back and bring Hector his report': *Iliad* 10.336–7, or 'Asios came near the ships: he was not after all going to return to windy Troy with the horses and the chariot he took such pleasure in': *Iliad* 12.112–15);

or it may underline a taunt ('so it wasn't after all a defenceless man's companions you were going to eat in your violence in your hollow cave', says Odysseus to the Cyclops after his escape and his blinding of the giant: *Odyssey* 9.475ff.). It may mark the pain of an unforeseen discovery ('Ajax,' says Odysseus in the world of the dead, 'so you weren't after all going to forget your anger against me for the arms you lost, ever, even in death': *Odyssey* 11.553ff.), or the blindness of a wish (Patroclus asks Achilles to be allowed to go and fight; 'the fool,' comments the narrator's voice, 'he was asking for what was to be his own grim death': *Iliad* 16.46ff.); it may be lighter in tone, as when a delighted Athena says to Odysseus, back in Ithaca at last, 'so you weren't after all going to forget your tricks, your fictions and your deceptions, then, even in your own country, you villain!': (*Odyssey* 13.293ff.). But everywhere 'he wasn't going to' is part of the storyteller's repertoire of devices to mark and underline the turns of his narrative. Even the appearance of inevitability may be misleading: 'ah, I was bound to [going to: *emellon*] meet the shameful death that Agamemnon met in his halls, if you, goddess, had not told me all these things as you should' (*Odyssey* 13.383–5), says Odysseus to Athena later in his conversation with her. Herodotus' use of the motif emerges as another Homeric reminiscence in his role as storyteller, like the phrase used of the twenty ships that Athens sent to support the Ionian revolt: 'they were the beginning of suffering for Greeks and non-Greeks alike' (5.97.3). When Patroclus, in the eleventh book of the *Iliad* (he dies in the sixteenth), hears Achilles' summons to see the wounded Greeks streaming back to the ships and comes out of the tent 'like Ares': 'that was the beginning of suffering for him' (*Iliad* 11.604) is the narrator's comment. Herodotus' sense of what was 'going to happen' is not the language of one who holds a theory of historical necessity, who sees the whole of human experience as constrained by inevitability and without room for human choice or human responsibility, diminished and belittled by forces too large for comprehension or resistance; it is rather the traditional language of a teller of tales whose tale is structured by his awareness of the shape it must have and who presents human experience on the model of the narrative patterns that are built into his stories; the narrative impulse itself, the impulse towards 'closure' and the sense of an ending, is retrojected to become 'explanation'.

The objection is to hand that that will not do. It will be argued that Herodotus does have a theory of history,[12] one which he enunciates in his own voice at the beginning of his narrative and which he several times puts into the mouths of wise men such as Solon or Artabanus, or into the mouth of the Croesus who survives his own downfall to become another of the wise.[13] In what is in effect a second preface, before starting on the story of Gyges and Kandaules, Herodotus sets out a general principle which, it seems, is to guide his whole work: 'I shall indicate whom *I* know to have begun the sequence of wrongs against the Greeks, and I shall go forward with my story, taking in small and great communities of men alike. For those that were great long ago, the majority of them have become small, and those that in my time are great were small before. Since I am sure that human achievement nowhere remains in the same place, I shall mention both alike' (1.5.3). What looks at first sight like a similar 'theory' of human history forms the introduction to Croesus' advice to Cyrus before his last battle with the Massagetae (advice which, incidentally, leads to Cyrus' defeat and death): 'If you acknowledge that you are a man and that those you command are men also, you must first realize that there is a cycle of human experience: as it goes round, it does not allow the same men always to succeed' (1.207.1). Earlier, Solon had given expression to another such general truth of human experience in his famous words to Croesus: 'Croesus, you question me on the experience of men when I am sure that divinity is altogether envious and disruptive. For in the long length of time one may see, and may suffer, much that one does not wish' (1.32.1). Solon goes on to declare that chance rules man in everything ('in everything man is chance': *symphore*; 1.32.4), and that no man, since he is a man, can have all the things that constitute happiness, just as no country has every natural advantage. We can hear an echo of Solon's words, six books and many years of narrative later, in words that Xerxes' uncle, Artabanus, speaks to him when Xerxes laments the shortness of human life after reviewing the vast expedition he has assembled for the invasion of Greece: 'Even in so short a lifetime,' Artabanus says, 'there is no man so favoured by the gods... that the thought will not come to him to wish, not once but again and again, rather to be dead than to be alive. The disasters of chance befall him; diseases bewilder and confuse him, and they make life, short as it is, seem long. This is how death comes to be a man's most desired refuge from the distress of living; even in giving us a taste of the sweetness of life god is found a jealous giver' (7.46.2–4). Other echoes appear in Amasis' advice to Polycrates ('divinity is envious': 3.40.2), and in Themistocles' attribution of the victory of Salamis not to human achievement but to the gods and heroes, 'who showed themselves envious that one man should make himself king of Asia and Europe, when he was moreover impious and wicked' (8.109.3).

But is this a theory of history, an 'historical philosophy', as Charles Fornara calls it?[14] Closer inspection suggests that we are not quite dealing with the sort of unified and structured set of ideas that we are entitled to call a theory, but rather with a set of metaphors of very different implications. A 'cycle' (*kyklos*) of human experience suggests regularity and recurrence as well as inevitability; the 'envy' (*phthonos*) of divinity seems to imply a pattern of supernatural intervention in human life which is itself recognizably 'human' in its motivation and hence once more in principle predictable. But 'disruptiveness' (*to tarachodes*) and the recurring idea of 'chance' seemingly stress the randomness and unpredictability of divine intervention, while the impossibility of a man's possessing all goods seems to point to something different again, something more like a natural limitation. Moreover, Herodotus' narrative itself only once directly suggests that divine envy may be responsible for what happens to man, and that is in the first book at the very beginning of the story of Croesus' downfall, where Herodotus offers, explicitly as a guess, the suggestion that the 'anger' of a god (Herodotus' word, his only use of it, is *nemesis*, which in Homer means something like 'righteous indignation' and has nothing at all of its modern associations) 'took hold' of Croesus, because he thought himself 'the most blessed of men' (1.34.1). That might perhaps be the 'envy' of divinity, but Herodotus does not call it so and in the context it might equally well be anger at Croesus' blind sense of invulnerability (what Shakespeare's contemporaries called 'security'), and the disregard for divine power that it implied. (It is perhaps necessary to add that what it is certainly *not* is divine punishment for *hybris* on the part of Croesus, as modern readers all too readily suppose: of *hybris*, as Herodotus understood it, there is no trace in the story of Croesus. Herodotus does not often use the word, and never of Croesus.) But in general it is true to say, as Mabel Lang has done recently, that divine envy 'has no merit for Herodotus as an expression of historical causation',[15] and that his narrative is very far from being constructed to reflect, let alone demonstrate, the existence of a 'cycle' of human experience.

His narrative does perhaps more clearly convey the idea that the most fundamental of all human disabilities is the inability, displayed by Croesus, to understand the nature of human experience – the assumption that nothing, not even a god, can destroy the power and prosperity of the great: that is Xerxes' disability, against which Artabanus vainly argues, and it is the disability also of Apries, the Egyptian pharaoh deposed by Amasis, who himself is the paradigm of a man profoundly aware of human vulnerability (2.169.2). But if that is a 'cause', it is one that sees human disasters as brought about by human shortcomings, not by supernatural causes such as 'divine envy'.

To understand Herodotus' thinking about divinity we need to distinguish between supernatural explanations of specific events which befall specific individuals, and a general theory of historical causation. In particular cases, Herodotus shows himself on occasion prepared to accept the anger of a supernatural power as explanation. The action of the Spartans in throwing two Persian heralds, sent by Dareius to demand submission, into a well to die is punished a generation later by the sudden and unexpected visitation of death upon the sons of the two Spartan heralds sent to Susa to offer themselves as substitute victims for this act of sacrilege. The offer of reciprocation is rejected by Xerxes, according to Spartan tradition, and the attribution of the sons' death to the anger of the hero Talthybius, patron and protector of heralds, is explicitly accepted by Herodotus: 'justice' required that heralds should pay for the death of heralds, but the chance that it was precisely upon the sons of the men who offered themselves as substitute victims that death came seems to Herodotus to show that this was divinity in action (7.133–7, esp. 137.2). In other cases there may be doubt and room for argument: so it is with the suicide of the Spartan king, Cleomenes (6.75.2; 84), or with the wrecking of the Persian fleet sailing round Euboea to take the Greek fleet at Artemisium in the rear (7.188–9).[16]

But these are specific cases and do not constitute a 'theory' of human historical experience at large. Before we attribute such a theory to Herodotus we need to consider the possibility that we have been misled by a formal resemblance between Herodotus' generalizations and the language of theory, and by our own ever slighter familiarity with the very different use of the language of generalization in the form of proverbs.

Herodotus' audience would have recognized his generalizations as *gnomai*: the Greek word *gnome* is not quite what we call a proverb (since it can be the creation of an individual on the spur of the moment), but like a proverb it will have the form of a generalization, a summing-up of human experience ('divinity is envious'); it will be offered as a truth to be acknowledged by its hearers, and which at a particular moment may seem to explain and pigeonhole some fact, action or event, and bring it within the bounds of meaning. It too represents an aspect of the impulse to narrate; it is another facet of the narrative contract between storyteller and audience which accepts by collusion the interpretability of experience. It is what Walter Benjamin calls 'an ideogram of a story': 'a proverb, one might say, is a ruin that stands on the site of an old story and in which a moral twines about a happening like ivy around a wall'.[17] What the proverb does not do, nor will it be supposed by its hearers to do, is require all subsequent experience to bear it out; it does not claim to put forward the sort of general truth that offers what one writer has called 'a sort of inferential licence', a hypothesis that is to be verified or falsified by the occurrence or non-occurrence of its predicted consequences; it is not an assertion that any counter-example will render void. It is in this sense that the *gnome* and the proverb are alike: if I say, 'He who hesitates is lost,' I am not asking to be rebutted by being faced with examples where quick decisions have led to disastrous results. Faced with these, I say, rather, 'Look before you leap,' or 'More haste, less speed.' 'Look after the pennies; the pounds will look after themselves' is not a 'theory' of economic behaviour like Keynesian or monetarist theory; it exists happily side by side with 'Penny wise, pound foolish', just as 'Too many cooks spoil the broth' does not exclude 'Many hands make light work.' They are what another recent writer has called 'refined common sense';[18] they are generalizations which permit contradiction and conflicting interpretations, but at the same time they appeal to accepted truth, to shared experiences and to the comfort of familiarity; in some measure they serve to produce a map of human experience. They are intelligible and they reassure.

If this line of thought is right, then Herodotus is not offering in his gnomic generalizations 'laws of history' to which all events must conform and which it is the function of his narrative to demonstrate; he is not offering an explanatory hypothesis of why things happen in human experience, on which we are to base historical inferences. As to that, his narrative offers us a different kind of explanation, with causes of another sort, in the form of human obligations and the predictability of their fulfilment. The function of his generalizations and his 'explanatory' truths is rather to relate what happens to the general fund of human wisdom.

The most pervasive strand of explanation in Herodotus' narrative, so pervasive that it constitutes the essence of his perception of events, is the sense that historical experience is the result of reciprocal action, the fulfilling of debts of gratitude and the taking of revenge. I have already suggested that we have no reason not to take revenge, and the 'who started it?' question, as perfectly serious issues.

Take, as one instance among many, the speech of the Scythian chieftains in 4.119.2–4: they are replying to an appeal from their more westerly neighbours for a common front against the invading army of Dareius. 'If it were not you who were the ones who committed the first wrong against the Persians and started warfare between you, then in asking of us what you now ask we would have thought you to be speaking quite properly, and we would now accept your request and act with you. But in fact you invaded their territory without our support, and you controlled the Persians as long as the god granted you to control them; while they, since the same god now arouses them, are now giving you the like treatment in return. We did no wrong to these men at that time, nor are we now going to be the first to attempt to wrong them. If they attack *us* and start on wrongdoing, we shall resist them; until we see this, we shall keep our distance. It is our belief that the Persians are not attacking us, but those who were responsible for the wrongdoing.' 'Responsible for' means 'having started'. The argument is not about who is 'right': it is taken for granted that both parties are doing 'wrong'; the serious question is 'who did the first wrong?'; 'who started it?' We can adduce the perhaps surprising parallel of the Nilotic Nuer, the subject of Evans-Pritchard's classic study of social structure: 'a Nuer dispute is usually a balance of wrongs, for a man does not, except in sexual matters, wantonly commit an act of aggression. He does not steal another man's cow, club him, or withhold his bride-cattle in divorce, unless he has some score to settle. Consequently it is very rare for a man to deny the damage he has caused. He seeks to justify it, so that a settlement is an adjustment between rival claims.... Nuer defendants are remarkable in that they very seldom lie in cases brought before government tribunals. They have no need to, since they are anxious to justify the damage they have caused by showing that it is *retaliation for damage the plaintiff has inflicted earlier.*'[19]

We should not be surprised; we should remember the frequency with which argument about 'beginning the hostility' and the necessity for revenge figures in Athenian law-court procedure. For a revealing example, we may take an argument

offered to a jury by the prosecution, in the opening paragraphs
of a speech attributed to the fourth-century orator Demosthenes. In this case the prosecutor opens the proceedings by
asserting that he and his family have been wronged by one
Stephanos: the alleged wrongdoing involved his brother-in-
law, his sister and his wife as well as himself as victims. He
goes on: 'so I am bringing this case not by way of starting
anything but to obtain my revenge: it was the defendant who
started our enmity, having previously suffered no harm from
us, by either word or deed.' He then proceeds to tell a long
story of how Stephanos brought a trumped-up charge against
him on which he was convicted, and then demanded of the
court a fine so immense that there was no possibility of his
being able to pay it, so that (under Athenian law) he would
lose all rights as a citizen. The ploy failed, as did another,
different but equally trumped-up charge. The prosecutor then
continues: 'Everyone approached me in private and urged
me to embark on revenge for what we had suffered from
him, and even insulted me with the suggestion that I was
no man if I did not obtain revenge for my sister, my brother-in-
law, and my niece and wife' (Demosthenes, 59.1.11–15). He
explains the particular case he is now bringing by suggesting,
among other things, that it is as nearly as possible the mirror
image of the hurt that Stephanos had tried to inflict on him.
The jury are expected, clearly, to respond sympathetically
to this explanation of the speaker's motives and to accept
revenge as an entirely serious and proper, even an expected,
ground for bringing a prosecution before the court.

We should remember too the existence of 'beginning wrongful violence' as an offence in Athenian law,[20] and the story
about Herakles in Apollodorus (2.4.9), where Herakles is
charged with the murder of Linus but is acquitted after the
citation of a 'law of Rhadamanthys' saying that 'whoever
defends himself against one who begins wrongful violence
and kills his opponent is not guilty of murder'. So it was
too in Athenian law.

But of course *we* find it immensely difficult to take such
an analysis of human behaviour seriously. For us, 'he started
it; no, I didn't, *he* did' is essentially a childish exchange (except

in the context of international relations), just as the assertion of an obligation to return wrong for wrong is immoral. But that is a bad reason for denying that such thinking is entirely serious in Herodotus, or for talking of 'superficial connections'. We should recall rather that such thinking has philosophical underpinning: we should compare the definition of justice offered by Polemarchus in the first book of Plato's *Republic* (*Republic* 1.331e.4–5) as 'returning/paying back/discharging [the Greek word is *apodidonai*] obligations'. Such a definition makes the 'who started it?' question entirely serious. The 'reciprocity model' is Herodotus' most serious model for explaining not merely human and divine behaviour, but also, as we shall see in the next chapter, physical phenomena such as the course of the Nile and Danube. So it is for the pre-Socratic philosopher Anaximander a model for understanding the 'justice', i.e. the reciprocation of aggression and counter-aggression in the natural order, as revealed in the cycle of the seasons or in the alternation of day and night (Anaximander fr. B1 DK).

Herodotus' use of revenge as a mode of historical explanation is thus grounded not only in the craft of the storyteller but also in the model of reciprocal action which is built into his sense of the world. Narrative and explanation are one in the sense that by virtue of its sheer sweep and complexity Herodotean narrative gives a quite new depth to our sense of why, in this instance, things happened.

5 Mapping Other Worlds

The reach and sophistication of Herodotus' thinking, as well as its limitations, are nowhere better seen than in his recording of distant places and alien cultures. Herodotus' enquiries led him to record not only those actions and achievements of men that astonished him, but also everything that was remarkable about those parts of the world into which his pursuit of the expanding power of the Persian empire took him. Observing and questioning and recording what he discovered, Herodotus reveals himself as a man of acute perception, astonishing breadth of imagination and open-mindedness and remarkable powers of analytical thought. One of the most astonishing passages, and one which displays the combination of observation and analytical reasoning at its most impressive, is his account of the historical geography of the Nile valley (2.5.1–2). He first records his opinion that, even without being told, a man of intelligence who used his eyes could infer that the soil of Egypt is the product of the Nile, since a day's journey out from the coast of Egypt if one takes a sounding one draws up mud and the sea is already only eleven fathoms deep. Later (2.10–12) he adds that he himself had thought that the land between the hills above Memphis must once have been an arm of the sea, 'like the areas around Troy and Teuthrania and Ephesus and the plain of the Maeander'. These are areas with rivers with only one mouth, and that much smaller than any of the five mouths of the Nile. He compares the geography of lower Egypt with that of the Red Sea and goes on (2.11.4–12.3):

> If the Nile were to divert its flow into this gulf, what is there to prevent it from silting up within, say, twenty thousand years? I myself would expect it to silt up within ten thousand. Why therefore in the time that had elapsed before I was born should not a gulf much larger than this have

been silted up by a river as great and as powerful in its effects as the Nile? So I believe what people told me about Egypt and myself am strongly of the opinion that it is so: I noticed that Egypt projects beyond the coast line on either side; that there are sea-shells visible in the hills and a crust of salt, clearly visible even on the pyramids; that the only hill in Egypt which is sandy is the hill above Memphis and that the soil of Egypt moreover is quite unlike that of the neighbouring countries, Arabia, Libya or even Syria, but is black and friable as if it were mud brought down from Ethiopia by the river, whereas Libyan soil is reddish and sandy and that of Arabia and Syria somewhat clayey and rather stony.

This is brilliantly observed and the observations are applied with a breathtaking capacity to envisage a historical process on a vast scale: we can legitimately compare Herodotus' ability to imagine a process taking more than twenty thousand years with other cultures' far more limited conceptions of temporal perspective: for example, the Nuer time-reckoning in which, as Evans-Pritchard demonstrates, 'the distance between the beginning of the world and the present day remains unalterable' at ten to twelve generations (since time is perceived in terms of the lineage structure of a clan),[1] and closer to home, the less than six thousand years that constituted, before Darwin and the discoveries of geology, the entire historical perspective of orthodox Christianity from the Creation to the present day. The relaxed open-mindedness that Herodotus displays in these chapters is, if anything, surpassed later (2.15–17) when he expresses his own opinion on the contemporary Greek controversy about the boundary between Asia and Africa ('Libya', as it appears in Greek texts). Those Ionians who made the Nile the boundary are commited, he argues, to three unacceptable propositions: that there was no country of the Egyptians until the delta silted up (or that, contrary to Egyptian tradition, there were no Egyptians); that Egypt is not one country but two; and that as well as Europe, Asia and Africa there must be added a fourth 'part' of the world, the Nile delta. He dismisses these propositions as absurd, and gives his own view: 'Egypt is that whole territory occupied by Egyptians, just as Cilicia is the country occupied by Cilicians and Assyria the country occupied by Assyrians; the only boundary in the true sense that I know between Asia and Africa is that made by the boundaries of the Egyptians.' Boundaries matter to Herodotus as we shall see, and they are most often marked by rivers, but he is not prepared to set aside common sense and reliable tradition to create a tidy scheme. The Nile is not the edge of anything; it is the centre of something else, the place where Egyptians live and, by their own traditions, always have lived.

Herodotus can apply the same combination of observation and common sense to the information he gets from others. He has heard stories from Scythians about land to the north of them where it was impossible to move or even to see ahead of one because of a downpour of feathers (4.7.3.). A little later he is describing the climate of the country to the far north of Scythia where there is continuous frost for eight months of the year, where nomadic hordes travel along frozen rivers, and where you cannot turn earth into mud by pouring water on it but only by lighting a fire; horses can tolerate this climate but not mules or donkeys (4.31.1–2). These reports suggest another line of thought to him; he reverts to the Scythian stories of a sky full of feathers, and goes on: 'My own opinion is that to the north of this country it snows continually, though less in summer than in winter, as you would expect; anyone, for example, who has seen a blizzard of snow at close quarters knows what I mean: the snow is very like feathers.'

Occasionally the application of observation and common sense to geographical reports that he cannot himself test out leads to Herodotus' rejecting traditions that are soundly based. He dismisses, for example, the Greek theory of melting snow in Ethiopia as the cause of the Nile floods as totally mistaken, though highly plausible (2.22.1–4): the winds that blow from the south are hot, not cold; no rain falls there and it never freezes; the men who live there have black skins because of the heat of the sun; and migrating birds such as cranes migrate there for the winter, while swallows and hawks live there right through the year. Snow on any scale would make all these things impossible. But for the most part he does not simply suppress what he regards as incredible; he records it, and he argues against it, as he does with the tradition that Phoenician ships had once sailed round the southern tip of Africa, starting from the Red Sea and returning to the Mediterranean by the Straits of Gibraltar. He records (4.31.1–2) the Phoenician story of winters spent in growing crops for the next summer's voyaging, and adds the one detail that he cannot accept, that as they sailed round the south of Africa they had the sun on their right – that is, to the north of them.[2] Fidelity of that order to the obligation he has imposed upon himself of recording 'what is said' is simply not compatible with the fraudulent misuse of other men's researches that some have believed they saw in Herodotus.[3]

But there is another side to Herodotus' response to geographical tradition and one that has great importance for understanding the way his mind works. Fiercely independent, critical, empirical as he is in his judgments, he is nonetheless, like any of us, the product of his time and his culture, and on more than one occasion we can see him all too clearly superimposing the grid of his own cultural preconceptions on the data he is considering, and perceiving only what that grid allows to show through. Another tradition of exploration that Herodotus has encountered comes to him at three removes (2.32–3; again the faithful precision in tracing back the chain of informants is characteristic): Herodotus reports a conversation with some men at Cyrene in Libya who tell him of a visit they once made to the oracle of Ammon in the Siwa oasis. There they had spoken to the local chief who told them of some Nasamonian tribesmen who had once come to the oasis and of the story they told. Some young men of their tribe, outrageous in their adolescent disdain of restraint, drew lots for five of them to venture into the Sahara and discover things more distant than anyone before them. The young men travel in a westerly direction across sandy desert and eventually catch sight of trees growing. When they try to pick the fruit growing on these trees, they are attacked by little men, 'smaller than average men', who capture them

89

and take them to their city. Neither party can understand the other's language. The city is across 'great marshes', and is inhabited by men equally small; past it flows a great river with crocodiles in it, flowing from west to east. The Nasamonian tribesmen eventually returned, reporting that all the little men were wizards. The Ammonian chieftain gave it as his opinion that the 'great river' was the Nile and Herodotus accepts the identification. His grounds for doing so are remarkable: they are explicitly an inference from the known to the unknown and involve an elaborate parallelism between Nile and Danube. Herodotus believes that the Danube rises in the Pyrenees and flows west to east, dividing Europe in two, until it reaches the Black Sea at the Milesian colony of Istria. Egypt, where the Nile reaches the sea, is 'more or less opposite mountainous Cilicia' and Cilicia is only five days journey from Sinope on the Black Sea; Sinope is 'opposite the mouth of the Danube'. Thus the Nile, as it divides Africa in two, is 'the equivalent of the Danube'! The assumption of north–south symmetry is not made explicit but provides the essential premise for Herodotus' argument to work: it is clear that it is a projection on to the spatial plane of the fundamental assumption of reciprocity which Herodotus and his audience shared, and did not therefore need to spell out – perhaps indeed could not have spelled out. Space conforms to an 'ideal' model of a complete whole which represents a prescriptive 'reality', whose validity is not called into question.

The model abhors a vacuum, so that when Herodotus is confronted with traditions which, however confused and conflicting, seem to suggest the existence of a people to the far north called the Hyperboreans, he is prepared to leave the question of their existence open, but adds, as a matter of certain inference, that if they *do* exist, then there is also another people to the far south, the Hypernoteans (4.36.1). This is often taken to be a *reductio ad absurdum*, but that is not quite how it reads in context. Herodotus first mentions the Hyperboreans in reporting (4.13, in indirect speech) the contents of a poem by Aristeas of Proconessos who, on Herodotus' reading, claimed to have visited the Issedones, a tribe to the north of Scythia, when 'possessed by Apollo'. Aristeas' poem told how the Issedones had been forced out of their territory by the one-eyed Arimaspeans, how they in turn had forced the Scythians to migrate southwards, and how the Scythians, by their pressure, had forced the Kimmerians who lived on the Black Sea to leave their territory.[4] The only people, as Herodotus remarks without further comment, to play no part in this chain of southward migrations are the Hyperboreans. Later (4.32–5) Herodotus returns to the Hyperboreans: there is no tradition of these people among the Scythians nor any other tribe in that part of the world, unless perhaps among the Issedones (presumably a reference back to Aristeas' poem). Herodotus doubts even this, since, if they were known to the traditions of the Issedones, they would be known also to the Scythians. However they *are* known to *Greek* tradition: they occur in the poetry of Hesiod and Homer (if Homer wrote the *Epigoni*, which Herodotus looks as if he doubts), and there is a mass of tradition about them among the people of Apollo's holy island of Delos. On Delos there is a story of sacred offerings wrapped in wheat straw which regularly arrived by a route which is traced back via Tenos, Euboia and the north of Greece to the head of the Adriatic, and thence by land eastwards to the Scythians and from them to the Hyperboreans. That is how they come now, say the Delians, but the first time they were brought by two girls, Hyperoche and Laodice, who came escorted by five Hyperborean men. The girls never returned but are buried on Delos ('the tomb is on the left as you go into the sanctuary of Artemis and there is an olive tree growing on it'), and they are commemorated by the locks of hair which the girls and boys of Delos dedicate at their grave. Even earlier two other Hyperborean girls, according to Delian tradition, had come to Delos before Hyperoche and Laodice brought the 'tribute' they had undertaken to give to Eileithuia in return for the gift of swift childbirth. The earlier pair are commemorated in a hymn by Olen the Lycian which the women of Delos sing when they 'collect for them', and which is sung also by other islanders and by the Ionians; ash from the offerings at the altar is scattered on their tomb, which lies 'behind the sanctuary of Artemis, facing east, very near the eating-house of the

Ceians'. The Delian traditions about the Hyperboreans are thus detailed and intricate and claim great antiquity (Arge and Opis, the first pair of girls, came to Delos 'at the same time as Apollo and Artemis'),[5] but Herodotus is clearly worried by the absence of any knowledge of them among those who should be their near neighbours. The one thing in this difficult and tangled tradition about which he shows no doubt is the existence of a balancing people in the south, if these northerners themselves exist.

Herodotus' account of geography, then, is a complex of several different kinds of data: personal observation, the evidence of other observers, inference, and the application, *a priori*, of an 'ideal' model of space. All of these exist side by side;[6] Herodotus is aware of the evidential difference between first-hand experience and the accounts of others (2.29.1; 2.99.1), but there is no sense that he feels there to be a significant distinction, let alone the possibility of contradiction, between such evidence and the application of a model. A passage in the third book perfectly illustrates the apparent seamlessness of Herodotus' geographical thinking (3.89–99).

After his record of the plot of the seven conspirators against the usurping Magi and Dareius' accession to the throne of Persia, Herodotus begins his account of Dareius' reign with a description of the administrative and financial structure which the king imposed upon the Persian empire, in the form of satrapies and their annual tribute obligations. There is uncertainty about Herodotus' sources for this information (he gives none himself) but there is no doubt that his account is based on reliable and detailed evidence, whether written or oral, and his list of twenty satrapies, their constituent peoples and their tribute assessments, as well as his account of other peoples more distant who made symbolic gifts to the king, has as good a claim to be authoritative as any other source.[7] The list leads without a break into a passage which declares itself an account of how the gold in which the tribute of the Indian satrapy was calculated is gathered, but which first describes at some length the culture of the various Indian tribes. When we return to the business of geography, we are in a world of gold-bearing sandy deserts inhabited by savage ants 'bigger than foxes, though smaller than dogs' into which the Indians make forays, riding a team of three camels, at the time of day when it is hottest and the ants are underground sheltering from the heat. This time of day, in the Indian desert, is in the early morning, 'from sunrise to the time when the market breaks up'; after that it gets cooler, until by about noon it is much as in other parts of the world, after which it continues to cool. The Indians fill sacks with the golden sand, and make off at a gallop, pursued by the ferocious ants when they smell the raiders and have had time to gather in force. Herodotus twice notes that this tradition is due to Persian sources, and one naturally supposes some doubt in his mind. But immediately, instead of expressing scepticism, he launches into a general reflection: 'The edges of the inhabited world have been given, it would seem, the finest things, just as Greece has been given the finest climate and the most temperate' (3.106.1). He goes on to establish the point by a consideration of India, Arabia and Ethiopia, the most distant parts of the world to the east, the south and the southwest (of the west of Europe he has no certain tradition to relate, save that tin and amber come from here, and of the north only that most of the known gold of the world comes from there). In India, however, all wild animals except horses are bigger than those found anywhere else and great quantities of gold come from there; strange trees grow wild and bear a crop of wool finer than sheeps' wool out of which the Indians make their clothes. From Arabia come amazing perfumes and spices, which are gathered by the natives in astonishing and dangerous ways: they have to contend with gigantic swarms of flying snakes, bat-like creatures which attack men's eyes and great birds that make their nests of cinnamon sticks on precipitous cliff-faces. Strangest of all are the sheep, found nowhere else: one species with tails at least three cubits long so that all the shepherds have acquired enough carpentry to make little carts that the sheep pull behind them to support their tails, and another with flat tails a cubit across. In Ethiopia there is also gold in abundance; there are great elephants and the men are the tallest, most handsome and longest-lived. Herodotus concludes his survey of the edges of the world

(3.116.3) by repeating that 'those countries which enclose and ring the rest of the world seem then to have those things which we think most beautiful and most rare'.

The model of a symmetrical world in which normality and balance at the centre are surrounded by the fantastic, the threatening and the beautiful at the extremities is nowhere more explicit in Herodotus, even though elsewhere he pours scorn and mockery on mapmakers who produce images of a circular world encircled by Ocean, 'drawn as perfectly as with a compass', and with Europe and Asia equal in size (4.36.2): there is no first-hand evidence for the existence of Ocean, he protests more than once (2.21 and 23; 3.115.2; 4.8.2; 4.45.1), and Europe is far larger than Asia, as he argues in Book Four (4.42–5). But the rather less geometrical version of a symmetrical and reciprocating world is, for Herodotus, so overwhelmingly persuasive, at the deepest levels of perception, in its match with the institutionalized reciprocity which defines his moral universe, that it cuts out any awareness of the circularity of the arguments that support it and instantly suppresses the first stirrings of scepticism that are evoked by the Persian tales of man-eating ants in the burning sands of India.

When it is a matter of Herodotus' perception of inhabited space it is not too hard to judge where empirical data and analytical reasoning shade off and give way to the prescriptive thinking involved in applying an 'ideal' model to the traditions that his enquiries have opened up for him. It may be useful to bear the results in mind when we consider Herodotus' accounts of other cultures.

Herodotus states his attitude to other men's ways in his final judgment on Cambyses (3.38). 'It is clear to me', he writes,

in every way that Cambyses went completely mad: he would not otherwise have attempted to mock rituals and customs. For if one were to put it to all men and require them to make a choice of the finest customs out of the whole range of customs, each community of men would consider the matter and choose their own: so much does

94

every community of men believe their own customs to be by far the best. It is not reasonable then that any man except one out of his mind would mock such things. That all men do think thus about the matter of customs one can judge from many different pieces of evidence, among them this. When Dareius was king he summoned the Greeks who were present at his court to ask them how much money they would take to eat their own fathers when dead, and they said that they would not do this for anything. Dareius then summoned those Indian tribesman called the Callatiae, who do eat their forebears, and asked them, in the presence of the Greeks who followed what was said through an interpreter, what money they would take to burn their fathers on a fire when they died. The Indians raised a great outcry and urged him not to utter such sacrilege. That is how strongly custom determines these things. I believe that Pindar was right when he wrote in his poem that custom is king of all.

The same acceptance that the traditions of one culture are not to be used as the basis for dismissing those of another forms the grounds on which Herodotus justifies his refusal to discuss the religious traditions of Egypt (2.3.2): 'I am not anxious to relate the religious accounts I heard from the Egyptian priests, other than the names of their gods, since I believe that all men have equal knowledge of these things'; he seems to mean that no man can claim to know more than any other of divinity. Of course, there are things that Herodotus has seen or been told of other cultures that arouse in him a powerful feeling of revulsion (such as the Babylonian tradition of ritual sexual intercourse at the temple of the goddess he identifies as Aphrodite: 1.199), but these are very much the exception. By and large Herodotus records in an objective and unprejudiced fashion, without evident sense of superiority and sometimes with explicit approval, a vast range of cultural behaviour among the non-Greek peoples he encounters or hears of from others.

We have already seen examples of his linking character and behaviour to environment; his account of Egypt is the most systematic attempt to relate culture to environment, and at the same time to see the apparently random traits of behaviour that he had observed as making sense in the light of some perceived principle of order, in this case inversion of 'normality' (2.35ff.).[8] He explains the length of his account of Egypt by saying that it has more astonishing things and more achievements that defy estimation than anywhere else. 'The Egyptians not only have a climate of their own which is different in kind and a river which shows itself quite unlike all other rivers, but the majority of the habits and customs which they have established are entirely the reverse of those of all other men' (2.35.1–2).[9] He goes on to list examples of this inversion, and the list gives evidence of systematic and detailed observation across a wide range of diverse activities: the women buy and sell in the market, while the men weave at home; other peoples bang the weft home to the top of the loom, the Egyptians to the bottom; men carry loads on their heads, women on their shoulders; women urinate standing up, men sitting down; the Egyptians relieve themselves in their houses, whereas they eat outside in the streets; there are no women priests of either gods or goddesses; sons have no obligation to support their parents if they do not wish to do so, while daughters must, without exception; the priests of Egypt shave their heads, where elsewhere they grow their hair long; elsewhere the close kin of the dead crop their heads short, in Egypt they grow hair and beards long; all other peoples live separately from their animals, the Egyptians with them; other men make bread of wheat and barley, which the Egyptians reject as humiliating – they make theirs of spelt; they work dough with their feet, clay with their hands; other men leave their genitals 'as they were born with them', the Egyptians circumcise themselves; other men sheet their sails outwards, the Egyptians inwards; the Greeks write and calculate on an abacus from left to right, the Egyptians from right to left; they have two different scripts, one called sacred, the other demotic. Herodotus asserts that the Egyptians are the most reverent of all men and continues with an account of the Egyptian priesthood and of Egyptian religious rituals which sees the opposition between clean and unclean as definitive of ritual practice: the priests wash their clothing, and themselves, repeatedly, several times a day; they shave their whole bodies every two days to avoid any possibility of lice and they explain circumcision as due to a preference for cleanliness over comeliness. Leguminous vegetables and bulls with even a single black hair are unclean: clean bulls belong to Epaphus and may be sacrificed once they have been meticulously inspected by a priest whose assigned task this is, and marked as clean with a clay sealing.

Clearly there are things in all this about which Herodotus is simply wrong, and other things in which he is mistakenly generalizing from inadequate observation, but we should be chary about attributing casualness of attention to him: his accounts of the process of mummification and of the crocodiles and hippopotamuses of the Nile (2.86–90; 2.68–71) show with what precision he could observe and record strange phenomena. But in any case what is far and away the most impressive aspect of his account of Egyptian culture is his capacity to perceive a cultural 'matrix'. It is hard to overestimate the feat of imagination involved in this reading of an order in other men's ways. Herodotus is struck first by differences in gender roles between 'all other men' (that is, Greeks) and Egyptians, and this leads him to other patterns of binary opposition, between 'inside' and 'outside', between 'hair long' and 'hair short'. Differences in the making of bread lead in turn to the opposition between 'hands' and 'feet', and the list ends with the classic oppositions of 'left' and 'right', 'sacred' and 'profane'. Equally striking is his grasp of the opposition between 'clean' and 'unclean' as the key to understanding Egyptian religion: here too he may well have misinterpreted much of Egyptian religious practice, and the idea itself may have come to him from Egyptian priests, but to perceive that the washing of drinking vessels ('not some, but all rinse them out every day'), clothing and the human body are all connected as aspects of a system of religious observance and related to the practice of circumcision is itself another remarkable achievement. That all this should have fitted also with Herodotus' model of a world in which things become progressively more strange as one moves outward from (Greek) normality at the centre will only have confirmed for him the rightness of his observations, but there is no reason to suppose that the idea of inversion was itself suggested to him by the model and not rather by the inversion of normality marked already for him by the observed behaviour of the Nile.

It is likely that it was the closed system that Herodotus encountered in Egypt, its unfamiliarity and the absence of borrowings from other cultures which enabled him to see order in what he observed. He is markedly less successful, not only in the many smaller-scale sketches of alien cultures that he offers in passing, but also in seeing any structural order in Persian culture, which was certainly much more familiar to him and which, moreover, being closer to the 'centre', had less reason to be 'abnormal'. Here too, unsurprisingly, Herodotus begins with the observation of difference (1.131ff.) – difference (though it only emerges in passing) from Greek normality. 'It is not their custom to put up statues or temples or altars; on the contrary they attribute childishness to those who do, I think myself because they do not treat their gods as human in nature as Greeks do. Their custom is to climb the highest mountains and make sacrifice to Zeus (they give the name Zeus to the whole circuit of the sky). They sacrifice to the sun and moon, and to earth, to fire, water and to the winds.... Persian sacrifice is as follows . ...: they do not make altars or light a fire before sacrificing, and they have no use for libations, flute-music, garlands or barley grain.' He goes on to note the use of myrtle to decorate the headdress of whoever sacrifices, differences between the content of Greek and Persian prayers, and details such as the placing of the sacrificial meat 'on the softest grass, most often clover, that can be found and spread underneath it'. The presence of a *magus* and his chanting of words that 'the Persians say' is 'a theogony' ends Herodotus' account of Persian sacrifice, and he goes on to note other examples of unGreek behaviour, the celebrating of one's birthday as the most important day of the year, the consumption of a great range of desserts with relatively few main dishes, and the custom of making important decisions twice over on successive days, once when drunk and the second time sober (or, as he adds, vice versa). He has other things to say: about Persian greetings, about their valuation of other peoples (inversely in proportion to their distance from Persia) and their adoption of other men's customs, about their education, about their reluctance to execute anyone unless a calculation of good and bad things done overall shows a clear excess of bad over good, and about their abhorrence of lying, their treatment of lepers (as men punished for wrongdoing against the sun) and their respect and reverence for rivers. The impression left is of a more or less random set of observations of Persian behaviour and miscellaneous pieces of information gathered from Persian sources, selected mainly for their oddity, and the impression is reinforced by a coda about things less publicly visible which describes the treatment of the dead (leaving the corpse to be savaged by dogs or birds of prey before embalming in wax and burial in the earth) and the unique habit of the *magi* in killing 'with their own hands' all living creatures (Herodotus specifies ants and snakes) except men and dogs. Herodotus has no key to an understanding of these things that he has often accurately observed: he shows no knowledge of ideology, of ancient Persian religious dualism (in itself so radically different from Greek religious ideas as to present a genuine opposition) or of the nature or iconography of Ahura Mazda.[10] So what he perceives has to be made sense of by reference to his own ideological categories and what is lacking is any true measure of the gulf separating the Persian world-view from Herodotus' own, or even the nature of the difference.

We can form some idea of how much distortion takes place in feeding one set of cultural symbols through the grid imposed by another, and at the same time perhaps avoid the temptation of supposing ourselves as moderns immune to this danger, if we turn to the account given of Herodotus' own world-view by his English commentators earlier this century: 'literary art with [Herodotus] is largely a matter of religious teaching. The history of nations is but the grand stage on which may be seen the workings of Divine Providence.... In Nature, indeed, God appears as a principle of order ([Herodotus] ii.52.1), and Providence is kindly in the balance it maintains

([Herodotus] iii.108.2), but the very principle of balance presses hard on the individual man. The doctrine of Nemesis is set forth in the story of Croesus in its crudest form; God will have none exalted but himself. It may seem strange that the piety of H. did not revolt from such a view of the Deity. But we must remember....'[11] I find it difficult to recognize any of the essentials of Herodotus' perception of the world in the capitalizations and abstractions, and the intrusive singular, which mark that account; and we should not suppose that Herodotus' own distortion of other cultures (or ours of his) is either less marked or less culpable.

It is in his account of the Scythians, the Massagetae and the Ethiopians that we find most strikingly the problem of assessing the true character of Herodotus' thinking and observation of other cultures. For Herodotus, it emerges, Scythia is the antithesis of Egypt: its people are, by their own account, the most recent of all races (by contrast with the Egyptians who, until Psammetichus, claimed to be the oldest: 4.5.1; 2.2.1); its landscape is vast in extent and featureless except for more than twenty navigable rivers, the greatest (apart from the Nile) and the most numerous to be found anywhere. Above all, by contrast to an Egypt where the building and engineering achievements of man are more numerous and more astonishing than anywhere else in the world, Scythia is marked by nothing that might even recall to subsequent generations the presence of human life or the history of human achievement (4.82; 2.35.1): no cities, no statues, no temples, not even the evidence of agriculture (the 'works of men', as Homer calls them). Instead men, their habitations and their livestock are always on the move, so that even their funerals take the form of travelling columns of men and wagons who move from one encampment to another for forty days. The only landmarks of human creation seem to be the burial places of the Scythian kings on the River Borysthenes, marked by great mounds, and the huge brushwood altars, six hundred yards square, in honour of the god that Herodotus identifies as Ares, the Greek god of war, surmounted by 'an ancient iron stabbing sword'. In keeping with this inhuman landscape Herodotus records only one achievement of the Scythians that displays more skill than that of any other human people (4.46.2): that is their ability to ensure, by their own nomadic way of life, that no one who attacks them can escape, and that no one can pin them down if they do not wish to be found. 'For the rest,' Herodotus adds, 'I do not like them': the Scythian denial of everything that men struggle for to assert their existence and their humanity arouses in Herodotus a response akin to fear. His account of their culture focuses on religion and on their treatment of enemies slain in war, whose skulls they scalp and whose entire bodies they sometimes skin. Though he identifies their principal divinity with the Greek goddess of the hearth, Hestia,[12] it is the sacrificial rituals in honour of Ares that Herodotus describes in most detail: as well as animal sacrifice, the ritual involves decapitating one out of every hundred prisoners of war, pouring the blood over the sword that crowns the brushwood mound, and cutting off their right arms at the shoulder, leaving it and the headless, armless corpses 'where they fall' as they move off. Herodotus describes the Scythians as intensely hostile to the customs of other peoples, above all to Greek customs, and supports his assertion with two stories of Scythian notables, one a king, who allowed themselves to get taken up with Greek culture, in particular religious ritual, and who paid for it with their lives (4.76–80). We might suppose in turn that Herodotus' picture of Scythian culture is the result of his applying his model of a reciprocating world, or simply of revulsion at a part of the world of which he knows only from the tales of travelling merchants, but for two things. Firstly, the fact that the Scythians, like the Massagetae and the Ethiopians, constitute a limit to the aggressive and expansive tendencies of the Persians, and in repelling the latter reassert the orderliness of the inhabited world; secondly, the clear evidence that he has seen for himself, and that he reports both what he has seen and what he has had described to him with faithful precision and a mass of detail. Not only is this clear from his elaborate account of Scythian royal burials, but also from the following account of behaviour that he clearly does not understand (4.71; 4.74–5).[13] After funerals, he says, the Scythians 'purify themselves': first they wash their heads, and then, after constructing a little tent of woollen felt, they place in it on a dish stones that they have made red-hot and scatter on to the red-hot stones the seeds of the cannabis plant. They then crawl inside the tent and inhale the smoke with howls of pleasure. Herodotus is entirely matter-of-fact about the cannabis – the Scythians make a cloth from the cannabis plant that only an expert can tell apart from linen; everything suggests that he has seen both the cloth and the cannabis smoking for himself, but he can read the latter only as a ritual purification by fumigation, as he says, 'of their bodies'.[14]

With the Massagetae and the Ethiopians we come to the extreme edges of the world. In Book Four the Massagetae figure in passing only as a tribe forcing the Scythians to migrate south across the Araxes by their pressure, but we have already met them as the last and fatal opponents of Cyrus in the first book (1.202–3). Herodotus' account of their country and of the way of life of the people who live on the Araxes is explicitly derived from hearsay: it includes stories of strange food and strange dyes, of sex had 'in the open like cattle', and of men sitting round a fire and inhaling the smoke given off by a 'fruit' which they throw on it until they are drunk with the smoke of it and begin to dance and sing. But his narrative of Cyrus' attack on these people is given as if at first hand. Cyrus first sends a false offer of marriage to the widowed queen of the Massagetae, who is not taken in. Seeing Cyrus' preparations for invasion, she advises him to 'rule what is his' and allow the Massagetae to control what they control (1.206.1). She offers him the option, if he refuses, of crossing the river unopposed to fight her on her territory, or of allowing her people to do the same. After debate, Cyrus crosses the river and destroys a large part of the Massagetae by a trick. He also captures the queen's son. Tomyris the queen sends him a final message (1.212.2–3):

Cyrus, insatiate of blood, do not be raised up by this success of yours, just because you have got the better of my son, not by strength in battle but by the fruit of the vine, a drug with which you fill yourselves also and become so insane that as the wine goes down evil words float up in you. Be advised and listen to what I say: give me back my son and go back out of my country unharmed; you have humiliated one third of the host of the Massagetae. If you refuse, I swear by the sun who is lord of the Massagetae that I will give you more blood to drink than you can stomach, insatiate though you are.

These two are matched, like heroes of the *Iliad*: there is a note of moral authority in Tomyris' reproof which is unmistakable to the reader who remembers Herodotus' report of Persian abhorrence of lying, but Cyrus does not remember; he ignores the warning, his army is defeated and he is killed. After the battle, Tomyris searches for his body, beheads him and plunges his head into a sack of human blood. The tailpiece to the story is a totally factual account of the culture of the Massagetae: their weapons of bronze and their ornaments and horse panoplies of gold, their sexual promiscuity, and their habit of eating their dead kindred along with 'other animal meat' as a mark of honour. 'They sow no crops but live off meat and fish, of which there is no lack in the Araxes; they drink milk, and the only god they revere is the sun, to whom they sacrifice horses: to the swiftest of divinities they present the swiftest of all mortal creatures' (1.215–16).

Just over a book later, the same passion for enlarging the boundaries of his power that had taken Cyrus to the far northeast takes Cambyses to the south-western edge of the inhabited world, to confront 'the long-lived Ethiopians' (3.17.1): the epithet has an almost epic ring in its formulaic recurrence and is theirs alone (it recurs at 3.21.3; 22.3; 97.2; 114). Like Cyrus, Cambyses prepares for his invasion by a lying trick: he sends an embassy bearing gifts to the Ethiopian king, whose true mission is to reconnoitre this fabulous land. Like Tomyris, the king is not deceived by Cambyses' offer of friendship and reciprocal obligation. To the speech of Cambyses' envoys he replies (3.21.2–3):

The king of the Persians has not sent you here with gifts because he sets great value on becoming my friend: you do not speak the truth (you have come to spy out my country), and he is not a good man. If he were good, he would not have conceived a passion for a land which is not his, and he would not be trying to make slaves of men who have done him no wrong. Give him this bow and tell him this: the king of the Ethiopians advises the king of the Persians, when the Persians can draw as easily as this, bows as great as these, then to send an army of superior numbers against the long-lived Ethiopians, and until then to thank the gods that they have not put it into the minds of the sons of the Ethiopians to seek to add to what they have, a land which is not theirs.

When the envoys explain to the king the process of dyeing that had produced the fabric which they bring for him, he comments that these are men who use tricks and that their clothes match them. Only the palm wine he approves, and suggests that without it men who eat dung would not live even so short a life as eighty years: the Ethiopians live to be at least a hundred and twenty, and they eat boiled meat and drink milk; they wash in water (report the spies) that smells of violets, leaves their skin gleaming as if they had oiled it and is of such low density that nothing would float in it. (If that is true and they use it all the time, Herodotus adds, that must be why they are long-lived.) This story, told partly in his own person, partly in indirect speech, ends with a description of the burial practices of the Ethiopians: they mummify the corpse, perhaps as in Egypt, cover it in plaster which they paint with as close a likeness of the dead person as they can achieve, and then enclose the whole mummy in a hollow cylinder of rock crystal which they keep in the house of the nearest kinsman for a year and then stand in various places about their city. The crystal enables the kinsmen to see as if the whole of the naked body of the dead without unpleasant smell or sign of putrefaction. When his spies carry this story back to him, Cambyses, in a sudden passion, decides on an immediate invasion of Ethiopia without allowing any time to require the collection of supplies and 'without reckoning that he was about to mount an expedition to the edges of the world' (3.25.1). The invasion is a disastrous failure:

food supplies run out before a fifth of the march is completed and, after eating the baggage-animals, the army resorts to drawing lots and killing and eating every tenth soldier of their own number. By the threat of cannibalism Cambyses is forced to abandon his attempted conquest and turn back.

Symbolic thinking seems to dominate the whole episode (3.22.1–25.7). Clearly we have a mirror image of the episode of the Massagetae: outdoing the Persians in violence is matched by outdoing them in restraint; a sack of blood is matched by a casket of crystal, promiscuity by purity, eating the dead as a form of social reincorporation by reincorporating their apparently living images into the community; both the queen of the Massagetae and the Ethiopian king assert and prove their superiority to the deceiving king of Persia. The 'edges of the world' repel the invading power of Persia, which is forced to withdraw within its own due boundaries, and the fact that Cyrus and Cambyses alike have to be forcibly confronted with the fact of an uncrossable boundary and that the death of each follows hard upon the confrontation is structurally opposed to the wisdom and understanding of limits displayed by Dareius in abandoning his attempted conquest of the Scythians before disaster compels it. Both Cyrus and Cambyses are structural prototypes for Xerxes, while Dareius is his foil.

So much seems simple to grasp, but the intricacy and fineness of Herodotus' thinking escapes such over-crude attempts to categorize it. It is true enough that it is shaped by the perception of polarities and symmetries, by the 'logic of polar opposition', as it has been called,[15] but that is only half the truth. Herodotus' application of a prescriptive model of inhabited space and of human culture has the same function, and is as easily misunderstood as his use of prescriptive *gnomai* to describe human experience by the measure of a general truth. In both cases the 'ideal' description defines an order and brings experience within the compass of intelligibility. In doing so it excludes the possibility of an arbitrary and meaningless randomness in the things that man encounters in the world, but it does so without thereby simply screening Herodotus from the perception of what is there.[16] We have to allow for the presence side by side within his text of things as they are – precisely observed, measured, counted and recorded – with things imagined in terms of a prescriptive order, whether that order is narrative or moral. The problem for the modern reader of Herodotus is to determine where one begins and the other ends, or even to know whether the distinction makes sense in the face of a perception of the world so finely meshed.

The ambiguities of the relationship between symbolic and empirical thinking, and of Herodotus' own moral perception of the world and the place of man within it, are well brought out by his treatment of the idea of boundaries and limits to human achievement. The 'outstanding works' or 'achievements' (*erga*) of men are central to his declared subject, and repeatedly, as in his accounts of Egypt and of Samos (2.35.1; 3.60.1), he justifies the length of his treatment by the scale and number of such achievements. Buildings, as with the temples, pyramids and labyrinth of Egypt, or the harbour mole or the Heraion of Samos, are unambiguously marks of what men can do and evoke no sense in Herodotus that any limit set for human achievement is being transgressed. So too with the artificial lakes and waterways of Egypt and the tunnel that Eupalinos drives through the mountain to bring water from a distant spring to the otherwise waterless city of the Samians (2.99.2–3; 101.2; 108.2–4; 149–50, 158; 3.60.1–2); these too are simply, but admiringly, classed as 'achievements' (*erga*), and this in spite of the fact that they involve tampering with boundaries between the wet and the dry, earth and water, set by nature. With other such examples of interference with boundaries Herodotus shows himself much less at ease. We have already had the sense that with the last acts of self-assertion of Cyrus and Cambyses natural limits had reasserted themselves to the cost of men's lives. Another passage that perhaps belongs in this connection is the strange coda to Herodotus' account of the edges of the world in Book Three (3.117). Without explanation, after his account of how the world is ringed and enclosed by places which contain the most beautiful and rarest of things, Herodotus goes on to tell of an area of mountains, surrounding a plain in the territory of the

Chorasmians, on the borders of their lands and those of four other tribes, out of which a great river called the Aces once flowed through five clefts in the range of mountains. But when the Persian king became master of this territory in the far north-east of his empire, the inhabitants found their whole way of life altered. The significantly unnamed king dammed the five openings in the mountain range through which the river had flowed and turned the upland valley within the ring of mountains into a 'sea' (Herodotus uses the Greek word *pelagos* which denotes a large, open sea: he uses the same word for the Nile valley at the time of the floods) and the land at the foot of the mountains into an unwatered tract. The inhabitants 'suffer a great disaster': in the winter, 'when the god rains for them as for the rest of mankind', all is well, but in summer when they have sown their crops of millet and sesame they have no water. They are forced to go, men and women together, to Persepolis and to stand at the king's gates, where they howl aloud until the king sends orders to open the dam for the tribe which has howled most loudly. When their land is watered, that gate is shut and another opened for those whose appeal is now the strongest, and so on until they are all satisfied. For this, Herodotus has been told and accepts, they must pay much money on top of their tribute assessment.

After that Herodotus resumes his narrative with the first act of violence of Dareius' reign, the execution of his fellow conspirator, Intaphrenes. In the context, the story of the death of the River Aces has a sinister and uncanny ring: man has usurped the prerogative of a god and other men suffer. It is a narrative of unmediated and meaningless power. Thinking of rivers, one remembers other places where man's treatment of rivers has an uncanny resonance or is the trigger for disaster: not only Cyrus crossing the Araxes, but also Croesus crossing the Halys and Xerxes the Hellespont. Xerxes' 'yoking' of the Hellespont (7.10.1–2) is explicitly connected by Artabanus with Dareius' 'yoking' of the Bosphorus and his bridging of the Danube when he set out on his unsuccessful invasion of Scythia. Artabanus recalls that he had advised Dareius against attacking 'men who had no city anywhere

in their country' and recalls too how Dareius' army was nearly
cut off by the breaking of the bridge. When Herodotus
describes the making of the Hellespont bridge opposite Abydos (7.33–7), he himself refers forward to the fact that, 'not
long afterwards', the Persian governor of Sestos was crucified
by 'Xanthippos the son of Ariphron, general of the Athenians'
at the same spot, for his sacrilege against the sanctuary of
Protesilaos (7.33 referring forwards to 9.116–20): the association between building the bridge and subsequent horrific
events 'at the same spot' is not just made by the modern reader.
The bridge was broken and destroyed by a great storm and
Xerxes had the Hellespont whipped; those who are given
this 'monstrous honour' (*acharis time*, literally 'honour without benefit', a contradiction in terms) are required to utter
'barbarous and impious' words as they lash the water, words
in which Xerxes describes himself as 'master' of the water
on which he inflicts 'just penalty' and which he describes as
a 'river of bitter, muddy water'. The making of the bridge
is described at length with detailed, prosaic precision but the
act has uncanny overtones. Both the setting out of the
expedition from Sardis and the crossing of the Hellespont
are accompanied by sinister portents and monstrous actions
(7.37.1–39.3; 57.1). Xerxes' other interference with the boundaries imposed by nature, the canal through Athos, is put
down by Herodotus to his 'grandeur' (7.24); he 'wanted to
make a display of his power and to leave a memorial of himself'. 'Leaving a memorial' is an understandable desire that
elsewhere carries the ring of Herodotus' approval, but Xerxes'
'memorial' is an ambiguous one. It recalls the ill-fated action
of the men of Cnidos in trying to defend their city against
Harpagus' army by making a canal across the peninsula on
which Cnidos stood and 'making an island of their territory'
(1.174). The work is doomed to injury: men are blinded by
the splintering rock; the occurrence seemed 'something more
than was to be expected and divine' and the Cnidians sent
to Delphi to enquire 'what opposes them'. The answer is given
'neither to wall nor dig the isthmus: Zeus would have made
an island had he wished'; the work is abandoned and the
Cnidians surrender to Harpagus without a fight.

The answer of the Pythia does not quite settle the matter: we remember the 'achievements' of the Egyptians. We are left with general truths which do not exclude the counter-instance, and with the inscrutabilities of Herodotus' text. The storyteller leaves us to make our own judgment, perhaps nowhere more clearly than with Cyrus' punishment of the Gyndes, a tributary of the Tigris. The Gyndes, as punishment for sweeping away one of Cyrus' sacred white horses, is reduced by him from a navigable river to an easily fordable stream by the device of drawing off 360 new channels (1.189). Cyrus uses his whole army in this operation, postponing his attack on Babylon for a year; thus 'the work [*ergon*] was achieved, though they spent the whole summer on it'. It is far from clear what sort of a 'work' we are to take this to be. The number, 360, signifies perhaps the days of the solar year (the white horses of the Persians were sacred to the sun), perhaps the degrees of a circle: is this an act of atonement, an 'achievement', or rather a display of petulance and power by man encroaching on the boundaries that set him apart from god? Elsewhere in his narrative Herodotus is not slow to make his approval and disapproval clear; he is not a 'disengaged narrator'. But here, perhaps, we are at the boundaries of his own judgment.

6   Reading Herodotus

Herodotus' model of a world which is structured spatially and socially by patterns of reciprocity, tending outwards from the norm of a central *ego* (which may be either individual or group – city, culture, people) and held together by a criss-crossing network of obligations, is the key to understanding his work as proto-historian. It both gives Herodotus a means of sorting and recalling information he has accumulated in vast quantities, and provides a model which can generate narrative on a historical scale, because the network of obligations flows through time by the mechanism of inheritance from one generation to another. It is not a closed system, since there is no reason why spatial and social reciprocities cannot be indefinitely extended, which is why Herodotus' world is both so open and expansive and so rich.[1] And the roots of Herodotus' enquiries, and hence of his text, in oral tradition gathered in face-to-face encounters, are the key to its perennial humanity. This, we see, is how human experience is remembered and communicated: the dialogues which distinguish Herodotus' text from that of Thucydides are the mark of that unmediated orality and constitute in some measure proof of its authenticity. But to grasp that Herodotean narrative is rooted in oral tradition is only part of what we need to do in order to understand and use him. It is vitally important also to register that Herodotus is at pains, at every point in the presentation of his narrative, to preserve the traces of his process of enquiry; his narrative, that is to say, incorporates indications of its own limitations as 'truth-telling'.

The point is crucial and has been well made in a recent essay by Carolyn Dewald, in which she draws attention to the 1,086 examples of Herodotus' authorial intervention as eyewitness, investigator, scrutineer and writer. Herodotus, as she suggests, is concerned to 'preserve the record of his

struggles with a difficult and problematic medium'. His 'contract with the reader' is constructed so as to 'thwart any tendency we might have had to fall under the spell of his *logoi*
and to treat them as straightforward versions of past events'.[2]
In this Herodotus is once more crucially and definitively different from Thucydides. Thucydides, apart from a methodological paragraph or two early on in his work, systematically
covers the traces of his own investigations and presents the
reader instead with narrative as a transparent medium for
incorporating the events of the past 'as they happened'. That
was a conscious and deliberate choice: Thucydides the historical investigator presents himself as having conducted his investigations in so rigorous a way as to render his account of
them magisterial and definitive: this is the end of investigation. He makes the point explicitly in commenting, on the
question of the causes of the great war between Athens and
Sparta, that he has recorded the disputes that led to the breaking of the peace treaty between the two cities, 'so that no
one need ever again investigate the cause of the outbreak of
so great a war between Greeks' (Thucydides 1.23.5). It is difficult to imagine a more unHerodotean remark.

Thucydidean narrative, in the very rhythms and texture
of its language, claims and enacts authority. Herodotean narrative, by the same criteria, is a very different thing: it retains
the rhythms and forms of oral tradition, familiar to us in
folk-tales and märchen, but at the same time incorporates
into the text, as folk narrative never does, its own authorial
commentary on the sources and truth-value of the narrative.
It is of the essence of the traditional tale that it presents its
world, however fantastic (talking animals, houses made of
sweets, giant beanstalks), as unquestionably real, even if time-
less: the world of the narrative is 'out there', if we have the
eyes of the storyteller to see it. Herodotean narrative, on the
other hand, speculates on the reality of the world it presents,
not only by authorial interventions and by constant references
to its sources, but also by such devices as the tale told in
indirect speech and by the presentation of alternative and
competing narratives.

That is both the mark of Herodotus' originality and the

cause of his problematic status for subsequent readers. For the 'problem of Herodotus', as we may call it, is not the invention of the twentieth century. Indeed it begins in the generation after Herodotus when Thucydides uses 'storyteller' and 'story-like' as pejorative terms, almost certainly with Herodotus in mind.[3] As Momigliano has shown in a classic essay, Thucydides' judgment has largely prevailed in the history of historiography, and Herodotus has been as often cast in the role of 'father of lies' as in that of 'father of history'.[4] Even when admired, he has been admired for his style, his charm or his grace, not for his use as historian. Thucydides decreed that serious history could not be written of things remote in time or space, but only of what could be verified by the cross-examination of eyewitnesses; 'intelligence from afar', the realm of the storyteller, was not its province, and with that judgment Herodotus becomes marginal to the main-stream of historiography and for the most part remains a marginal figure until documentary history begins to be written in the nineteenth century.

The question, of course, is the question of how we are to read Herodotus or, to put it in more authorial terms, how we are to interpret his purpose in writing. Walter Benjamin, in the essay of 1936 on Nikolai Leskov from which I take my epigraph, has argued that we are less and less able, not merely to tell a story, but also to understand and respond to the craft of the storyteller. Perhaps because storyteller and historian have, at least until recently, shared a common narrative mode of presentation, the possibility of confusion about objects and methods is always to hand. Historians in particular are liable to be led into misreading Herodotus by their common assumption that the business of reading him has to do with prising loose 'historical facts' from the storyteller's narrative, and with substituting 'historical causes' for the storyteller's 'narrative devices'. Where there are no 'facts', there are 'lies' – false assertions about the events of the past which it is the reader's business to identify and erase from the historical record. In the process it becomes difficult, even impossible, for us to use Herodotus for what he is.

Let me illustrate the point from the work of two distinguished modern students of ancient history. A.W.Gomme, in an essay on 'Herodotus and Marathon' which begins 'Everyone knows that Herodotus' narrative of Marathon will not do,' puts forward suggestions for interpreting the Herodotean narrative in the light of its presumed basis in eyewitness accounts, so as to provide a probable account of what actually happened to precipitate the Greek attack and in the subsequent course of the battle. The resulting narrative is in crucial respects different from the one given by Herodotus. Gomme justifies his procedure by writing: 'this theory explains best the obvious mistakes in Herodotos' narrative ... [whereas] if we despair and say, "We know nothing of the course of the battle," in those words we are equally condemning Herodotus, saying that he made even greater mistakes than I have supposed, and that *his account is nothing but a fine piece of writing without historical value*.'[5]

My second example concerns the fall of Babylon in 521 BC, as related by Herodotus at the end of the third book. I suggested earlier (p. 23 above) that this story may be one of several that Herodotus derived in Athens from the Persian exile, Zopyrus, the grandson of the protagonist of his story. This possibility has recently been doubted by D.M.Lewis in the course of his illuminating essay on 'Persians in Herodotus'.[6] The grounds for this doubt are significant: they are that a nineteen-month siege of Babylon and the exploits of Zopyrus the elder as narrated by Herodotus are incompatible with the Persian, Babylonian and Aramaic evidence ('with the facts' is the significant formulation) which record Intaphrenes, not Zopyrus, as the Persian credited with the capture of Babylon, show no sign that Zopyrus was ever governor of Babylon, and no trace of a revolt lasting nineteen months very early in Dareius' reign but rather a pair of revolts lasting between them some five and a half months. As a consequence, Herodotus' story of Zopyrus' feat is false; it is another 'mistake' (what a less sympathetic critic would call another 'lie'), and *therefore* no longer something that we can use historically; further, Zopyrus the younger cannot be Herodotus' source for his account of the fall of Babylon. I have suggested earlier that, family traditions serving the purposes that they do, the last point does not follow from the premise that the story is false. The point I wish to concentrate on now is the further suggestion that Herodotus' story is a transformation (if you like, a falsification) of the past, transmitted through the oral tradition of Zopyrus' family, and that that transformation is itself a 'historical fact' as much as the two revolts of 521 BC described in the Behistun inscriptions.

Gomme himself, apropos of the famous speech in which Miltiades appeals to his fellow general Kallimachos to decide for freedom rather than salvery comments: 'Psychologically nothing could be better than that speech ... what would the decision be? Kallimachos decided for Miltiades and Athens and so Greece and all that Greece stood for were saved. That is how *Herodotus* saw the event.'[7] I think we can go further and say, this is how the generation of Herodotus saw the past; it is with the perception of the past by fifth-century Greeks that we are dealing in the text of Herodotus and that perception is itself a significant part of 'history'. Only by reading Herodotus in this way can we make proper use of Herodotean storytelling as history. Otherwise the text of Herodotus becomes for us merely a 'source' for something else, and one which in the judgment of many ancient historians is systematically flawed and unreliable.

The situation is much the same when it comes to causation. In another admirable essay, on the causes of war in ancient historiography, Momigliano observes that ancient historians are generally less adequate in their analysis of the causes of war than in their accounts of political change and revolution. He connects this inadequacy with their acceptance of war 'as a natural fact like birth and death about which nothing could be done', whereas political structures were made by men and could be changed by men, so that the study of political change was both possible and profitable, while the aetiology of war was beyond investigation. This mode of thinking, in being blind to 'all-pervading economic, social, religious and psychological factors', displays the 'characteristic features of a more primitive way of thinking' which became outmoded at the same time as 'classically inspired constitutional theory came to an end', in the nineteenth and twentieth centuries.[8]

In this analysis there is much that is persuasive: Momigliano himself indeed treats Herodotus as among the least inadequate of ancient historians in understanding the causation of war, less inadequate for example than Thucydides, because of his more open mind and wider mental horizon. And it is certainly true that for Herodotus war, like other forms of conflict, is a fact of human experience. Yet somehow, with Herodotus, I feel that Momigliano's analysis misses a central and crucial point. The storyteller's mode of presenting human experience has no language in which to express abstractions such as 'underlying factors', other than the language of personification. The storyteller's business is the business of experience and that experience is the experience of persons; causation, as we have seen, is perceived as the exchange of personal motivations. In an essay already referred to, Jacqueline de Romilly draws a contrast between Herodotus' formulation of Sparta's motives for intervening in the affairs of Samos (3.47: revenge for the theft of the great bronze krater intended for Croesus and of the magnificent cuirass given them by Amasis) and the account of that formulation offered by a modern commentator, as a desire to 'punish Samian piracy'.[9] As she says, the difference in expression is revealing, and the point is well taken.[10]

It is not that Herodotus can perceive only the particular and has no room for the general. The texture of the story-teller's narrative is loose enough to accommodate generalization of experience, but the generalizations themselves are formulated in terms of persons. So, for example, when Artabanus warns Xerxes, after the review of his forces at Abydos in the seventh book, against the dangers of failure that even so vast an expedition must face (paradoxically the greater for the very size of the expeditionary force), he draws attention to aspects of Xerxes' situation which we might phrase as abstract 'factors': the absence of adequate harbours to shelter from storm the huge fleet that Xerxes has assembled, and the logistical problems of feeding and watering the enormous number of men who comprise the invasion force. But in Hero-dotus' narrative the dangers are, significantly, phrased as *personal* antagonists: 'you have against you', says Artabanus, 'the two most powerful enemies', and when Xerxes expresses his astonishment that any enemy could withstand his over-whelming superiority of numbers in men and ships, Artabanus specifies the 'enemies' as land and sea (7.46–52: Artabanus' words are in 47.2 and 49). This is not a matter of 'narrative convenience' or of 'style', but a mode of perceiving human experience, and if we classify that mode of perception as 'primitive' historiography, then we are in danger of losing the ability to make use of Herodotean narrative, directly and immediately, as history. It is perhaps an aspect of that mode of perceiving experience that leads Herodotus to feel the inadequacy of a purely 'abstract' grasp of experience. So, when he gives general form to his sense of the rightness of the Athenian decision not to contest the command of the Greek fleet at Artemisium, in a passage (8.3.1) which I have already quoted, his words mean literally 'division within the tribe is as much worse than war of one mind as war is worse than peace'. Although 'worse' is neuter in Greek ('a worse thing'), the adjective 'of one mind' seems to make war and conflict alike into aspects of experience that can be confronted as persons: even the use of metaphor is a comparative rarity for Herodotus. One is reminded of Croesus' words to Cyrus: 'No man is so far out of his mind that he would choose war in preference to peace: in war, fathers bury their sons; in peace, sons their fathers' (1.87.4). The unnaturalness of war is expressed as the experience of persons.

It is, I think, the desire to reclaim Herodotean narrative for 'history', from which his 'mistakes' and his 'primitive' conception of causation threaten to exclude him, that accounts for two widespread readings of his text. The first sees his purpose as essentially didactic, to present a narrative of the past as a kind of allegory in which, by substituting 'Greeks' for 'Persians', his fifth-century audience can read a message relevant to their contemporary political situation; on this reading, the overreaching of Persian imperialist expansionism and its defeat has a meaning for fifth-century Athenians from which they can come to understand how they cannot avoid repeating in their own experience the disasters of the past. The second reading sees Herodotus as escaping, in his later books, from the 'primitivism' of mythical versions of human experience, both in the form taken by events and in their causation, which dominates his first four books, into a truly historical perception of the events of the Persian wars proper in his last five books. I want to argue against both readings.

What I have called the didactic reading of Herodotus (which its proponents would prefer to call 'dramatic' or 'ironic') has its roots in the observation that Herodotus' attitude to the Athens of Pericles, the Athens contemporary with his own writing, is highly ambivalent;[11] not just in his explicit comments on Athenian democracy (to which I have already referred on p. 15 above), but also in several references to conflict between Athens and Sparta over control and 'leadership' in Greece and to the sufferings and misery created by such conflict (8.3.2; 6.98.1–2; cf. 5.93.1–2). These are, of course, references to 'later' events, as he himself says – later, that is, than the events of the Persian wars, ending in 479 BC, with which his own narrative in the later books is concerned. In the light of them, the sole and passing reference to Pericles himself (6.131.2; for the lion, cf. 5.92.3), which indentifies him as the 'lion' to which his mother dreamed she would give birth, takes on a profound aura of ambivalence. If we recognize that Herodotus viewed Periclean Athens ambivalently, so the argument runs, then other passages, less explicit, take on new meaning. In particular, Herodotus' treatment of Themistocles and the Spartan regent, Pausanias, can be felt as profoundly ironic. In both, though there is no explicit reference to their later disgrace and downfall, Herodotus' account draws the attention of an alert reader to the seeds of these events in the case of Pausanias, by pointed and detailed reference to his fascination, after the battle of Plateaea for which he is given striking, almost extravagant praise, with Persian wealth and conspicuous extravagance (9.82); in that of Themistocles, to his ruthless attempt to force the island of Andros and other island communities into contributing money to the Greek fleet (8.111–12; to be read in the light of 108.5, a reference forward to Themistocles' later fate). In each case, the end is hinted at though it lies outside the scope of Herodotus' narrative, and the narrative itself is to be read in the light of that end. In this way, Solon's words to Croesus ('look to the end': 1.32.9) become programmatic for the whole, and implicit in them is the tragic inevitability not just of the downfall of Pausanias and Themistocles but also of what Herodotus saw in his own day, the transformation of Athenian resolve and determination, which in 480 had saved Greece from the Persian threat (7.139), into becoming itself a threat to Greek freedom and the cause of unavoidable conflict and suffering. The technique of ironical foreshadowing has one of its most striking instances in the words that Herodotus attributes to the Sicilian tyrant, Gelon, in reply to the refusal of the Athenians to allow him to command the Greek forces against Xerxes in 480: 'Since you insist absolutely on having all, you cannot too soon return to Greece and tell them that the spring has been taken from the year' (7.162.1): the words are those that Pericles used in his speech over the dead of the first year of the great war with Sparta in 430 BC.[12]

This reading of Herodotus, with its premise that 'his history was born out of his passionate involvement in the great crisis of his time',[13] sees his purpose in writing as that of delivering a message to his contemporaries about themselves: in reading him they were to perceive implied in his narrative the transformation of the so-called Delian league against Persia into the empire of Athens, the forcible reduction of rebellious 'allies' and finally the outbreak of inevitable war between Athens and Sparta, the leading Greek states of his narrative; and they were thus to understand the necessity of that war and to recognize, in the light of the patterns revealed by Herodotus' narrative, the inevitability of history thus repeating itself.

The view that I have been summarizing is essentially that of Charles Fornara, but in a more general form the view that Herodotus sees himself as addressing his own contemporaries about their own experience seems to have become almost canonical: it is shared by no less than five of the contributors to a recent volume on 'Herodotus and the invention of history' and, in the form of an analysis of Herodotean narrative as political thought, is the basis for one of the most impressive essays in that volume.[14] I should not want to say that at some level of consciousness Herodotus did not perceive the events of his own lifetime as somehow falling into the same pattern as the events of two generations earlier that he was engaged in narrating, but to see that parallelism as forming the 'message' of his work and the reason for his writing is to focus the reader's attention on things that are peripheral to Herodotus' purpose and to preclude understanding of the tradition in which he sees himself as working. It implies that Herodotus' obligation in writing is to his contemporary readers and (in spite of Fornara's careful distinctions) it makes his purpose closely parallel to that of Thucydides, in that they both see the narrative of past events as justified by present or future understanding of human experience. That is not quite what Herodotus himself says, and the difference is an important one. In his introductory sentence, he implies firstly that the obligation he is discharging in writing is to the heroic figures of his own narrative, and secondly that the justification of his narrative lies in its function of preserving the human past from oblivion, from being simply erased from memory by the passage of time: '[I write] so that what men have done should not be obliterated by time and that great and astonishing achievements . . . should not be without renown.'

These perceptions ally Herodotus not with Thucydides, for whom the function of historical writing was to make human experience intelligible to future generations, but with Homer. It has been pointed out how closely the opening chapters of Herodotus' *History* repeat the pattern of the opening of the *Iliad*,[15] and the point has been stressed again recently by Gregory Nagy in an essay presenting Herodotus as the representative of a tradition parallel to that of Homeric epic, a prose tradition which, like epic, has the function of preserving and incorporating the 'renown' (*kleos*) of heroic actions.[16] The point that I want to stress is that Herodotus sees himself as discharging a debt owed to the past: without his discharging of that debt, the past would literally vanish since there would be none to remember it, and with that oblivion great men and great achievements would be as if they had never been: in place of the memory of them, the past would be a vacancy, a blank. And if that is the debt owed by the present to the past, it follows that the future has the same duty to remember the present: that is to say, Herodotus is fulfilling the role of memorialist, without whom human achievement has no existence outside the present. That perception of his role is very different, therefore, from Thucydides' perception of his, and relates Herodotus not only to poetry (to the poetry of Pindar, for example, as well as to that of Homer) but to an awareness of the brevity and precariousness of human achievement that is part of the deep consciousness of illiterate cultures.[17] It is an awareness that we find difficult, in a world of books, of film and video archives and of data banks, to recapture, and it is precisely that difficulty that suggests an alternative reading of Herodotus, one which gives him a role like that of Thucydides, which we find it easier to understand and which we take more seriously. But if we do that, we seriously misunderstand the intent of Herodotus' *History*.

In saying this I do not mean to suggest that Herodotean narrative has no meaning, or to imply a distinction between narratives with meaning and narratives without: the notion of 'meaning' is perhaps built into the very definition of a narrative. Rather I want to distinguish between the meaning of Herodotus' narrative (a meaning implicit in its shape as 'story') and Herodotus' conscious perception of his purpose in writing, and to suggest that in calling this perception 'primitive' and Thucydides' different perception 'sophisticated' we blind ourselves to the real sophistication of Herodotus' thought. As to meaning, I would want to say this: just as the *Iliad* is not a poem with a 'moral' but a moral poem (in the sense that it prompts us to think seriously about issues of morality, and that we cannot read the story attentively without so thinking), so Herodotean narrative prompts reflection about the nature of political action without having that reflection, in the form of a message, as its pre-existing cause.

The other half of Herodotus' preamble to his *History* commits him, as we have seen, to demonstrating the 'cause' of conflict between Greeks and non-Greeks and perhaps also, since the Greek word has both references, to assigning 'responsibility'. I have argued that he sees that 'cause' as the reciprocal action and counter-action of human beings and therefore as located in the most fundamental aspect of human behaviour, of society and ultimately of the world itself in its ordering. Herodotus traces back the causal chain to its starting-point in the aggressive acts of Croesus against the Greek cities of the Aegean coast and this chain, to all appearances, reaches back unbroken. But to many modern readers this appearance of seamless connection reaching into the past is illusory: Herodotus' narrative, they feel, has welded a 'primitive' mythical mode of explanation embodied in the stories of his earlier books on to the genuinely historical explanations of his later books; his whole perception of causation alters and with it his (and our) sense of the nature of historical action. This is the second misreading of Herodotus on which I want to say something.

The contrast I have been describing is commonly drawn in terms of the differences between Herodotus' accounts of Croesus and of Xerxes.[18] In the case of Croesus, it is argued, the tragic experiences, disastrous decisions and eventual downfall of a certainly historical king are presented as the working out of supernatural causes: the anger of a god, and the fulfilment of the prophecy that the wrong done by Gyges would be repaid in the fourth[19] generation (1.34.1; 1.13.2 with 91.1). Croesus' downfall involves the double intervention of Apollo himself (1.91.2–3), is accompanied by prophetic dreams, omens and riddling oracles, and is foreshadowed years before in the words of Solon that Croesus recalls when face to face with death on the pyre (1.86.3–5, recalling 32.1–9); the whole has a clearly paradigmatic function and exemplifies in its purest form magical thinking about the human condition and the employment of what Evans-Pritchard called 'mystical notions'.[20] By contrast, it is said, the story of Xerxes' decision to invade Greece and of the disastrous failure of his expedition is presented in Books Seven to Nine as the result of purely human miscalculation of a highly complex problem: his decision is taken after detailed and lengthy discussion with his advisers of the issues involved, and his failure is presented as the result of successive strategic and tactical errors and is attributed, where it is not a matter of ill luck, to the superior powers of resistance displayed by the Greeks, which Xerxes systematically underestimates. The narrative is political and military history in the strictest sense and the explanations of events are based on empirical observation and rational analysis of the factors involved.

In reply to this argument it needs to be said, firstly, that the distinction is overdrawn. Croesus' decision to invade the territory of the Persians is also presented as one based on rational calculation and humanly intelligible motivations, and Croesus' downfall too is attributed to tactical error and to his opponents' superior military skills: he fails to win the first battle with Cyrus because his troops are outnumbered and night falls before either side has gained the victory (1.76.4–77.1); the second battle takes place before Croesus, who had expected a lull in the fighting until the following spring, has had time to marshal the allied army of Egyptians, Babylonians and Spartans which he summons to assemble four months later (1.77). In this battle Croesus' cavalry are routed when their horses stampede because of their fear of the camels that Cyrus, on the advice of Harpagus, has stationed in front of his own cavalry, with infantry to separate the camels from his own horses (1.80). The Persian siege of Sardis that follows is succcessful because an observant Mardian in Cyrus' army notices that it is possible to climb the undefended and supposedly impregnable cliff of the acropolis above the Tmolus river: he watches a Lydian climb down the cliff to recover a fallen helmet, and make his way back up (1.84.2–5).

Conversely, the contrast plays down, if it does not ignore, the supernatural aspect of Xerxes' invasion of Greece. Here too the decision to invade is finally enforced, after conflicting debate, by supernatural visitation, in the form of the dream which I discussed earlier (p. 70f. above), and the invasion itself and Xerxes' defeat are accompanied by repeated omens, portents and storms which may be the expression of divine anger, and by similar riddling oracles: there is an eclipse of the sun as the army sets off from Sardis (7.37.2); a mule with two sets of sexual organs, one male, the other female (the female above the male), is born while the army is at Sardis (7.57.2); and as the army leaves Abydos after crossing the Hellespont a mare gives birth to a hare (7.57.1). As the Persians approach Delphi there is a miraculous avalanche, weapons dedicated within the temple of Apollo are suddenly found lying outside the building and a battle-cry is heard from inside the temple of Athena Pronaea (8.37); before the battle of Salamis the sacred olive tree on the acropolis of Athens produces a fresh shoot more than a foot long on the day after the acropolis was sacked and burned (8.55), and Dikaios and Demaratus see a vision of the Eleusinian procession on the plain of Thria (8.65); on the day of the battle itself a ghostly ship is seen (according to one tradition) by the Corinthian squadron and a ghostly voice heard by the whole Greek fleet, abusing them for their cowardice in backing water before the Persian attack (8.94.2–3; 84.2).

These are examples enough to show that the contrast between Herodotus' two narratives, of Croesus and of Xerxes, is not as absolute as some critics have wanted to suggest. Nonetheless the impression remains that some significant change of atmosphere separates the later books from the earlier. It is not necessarily a change that would have been evident to Herodotus: I have already drawn attention to the presence side by side in the person of Harpagus the Mede of the 'mythical' motif of eating his own son's flesh in ignorance, and of the 'historical' action of commanding the army of Cyrus which reduced, one by one, the Greek cities of Ionia, the Carians, the Caunians and the Lycians (1.118–19; 162–76).

But there are two respects in which Herodotus will have felt a difference between what he knew of Croesus and the information he had of Xerxes. The first is in essence a simple consequence of the difference in historical perspective: for the events of the 480s Herodotus could question eyewitnesses or at worst the children of eyewitnesses; for Croesus he had to rely on traditions descending through three or four generations. We should expect as a result that he had very much more information about Xerxes than he had about Croesus,[21] and we can test that *a priori* hypothesis against Herodotus' knowledge of the entourage of both kings. In the case of Croesus Herodotus knows only of a solitary Lydian adviser, Sandanis (1.71.2–4), and of a handful of visiting Greeks who

pass through his court: Solon, Pittacus (or was it Bias?), perhaps Thales. For the rest Croesus appears as a man acting
alone, progressively more and more isolated: he loses one
of his two sons (the other being dumb), his Phrygian *xenos*,
Adrastus (the inadvertent killer of his son), and finally his
brother-in-law, Astyages, overthrown as king of Media and
kept a prisoner by Cyrus. By contrast, Xerxes is seen throughout the narrative surrounded by kinsmen, vassals and
advisers, whose names, interrelationships, marriages and
intrigues are all known to Herodotus on the basis of good
evidence:[22] his extended family supply him with satraps, army
commanders, envoys; and beyond them he has close contacts
with Greeks such as the deposed Spartan king Demaratus,
who travels with him on his expedition, and other exiles such
as the Athenian family of Peisistratus. Xerxes thus appears
to the reader as a political despot at the centre of a great
political and administrative network of kinsmen and subordi-
nates whose functions in his service are seen in circumstantial
detail, and with lines of communication which extend his
power to the far reaches of the known world. The result
is that his actions are inevitably perceived in a wholly different
light from those of Croesus: his world is tangibly different
from that of the Lydian king, whose total isolation is finally
acted out in his standing in fetters upon the pyre, face to
face with death. The detailed grasp of the power structure
of Xerxes' court and administration displayed by Herodotus
is a more detailed and more densely populated analogue of
his understanding of the entourage of Dareius, where his
sources give him accurate information on the six families who
were descended from Dareius' fellow conspirators in putting
down the revolt of the Magi and who supplied him with
officials and commanders, as well as of the complex administrative structure of the empire.[23] Before Dareius, on the other
hand, Herodotus' knowledge of the kings of Persia and Lydia
becomes steadily more sketchy: Cambyses, Cyrus and Croesus are seen in a light which makes them seem progressively
more isolated.

The second respect in which Herodotus will have perceived
Croesus differently from Xerxes derives from the nature of

the traditions which he received about the two men. Both suffered an extreme reversal of their fortunes which for contemporaries will have been unexpected, but for the rest oral tradition recorded Croesus as a pious man, famous for his fabulous dedications to the gods and fabulously generous also to those who were his benefactors and came to his court,[24] while Xerxes was seen for the most part as a cruel and ruthless intriguer with no regard for religion. In consequence, the downfall of Croesus presents problems for Herodotus which that of Xerxes does not create: a good man, albeit one misguided in his sense of his own invulnerability, is reduced from a position of vast wealth and power to one of powerless vassal, effectively a prisoner of the Persian king; in his own words, the slave of his overlord (1.89.1). Significantly, Herodotus makes him more profoundly and swiftly aware of his own change of status than his conqueror, Cyrus: when Cyrus tells him that the Persian troops are looting his city and carrying off his wealth, Croesus replies, 'Your wealth and your city, sire: no more do I have any part in them' (1.88.2–3). But Croesus' downfall is a scandal and an outrage to Greek perceptions of the moral order; as it stands, it is inexplicable: why such a man? A more than human explanation is required for such threatening catastrophe. For Xerxes the participation of 'some god' in his fatal decision is merely one strand in the complex of causation, where for Croesus it is the last and necessary word.

These then are two aspects of difference between Croesus and Xerxes which, along with the narrative instincts of Herodotus as they work on the information that he has available, account for the reader's sense of moving in two different worlds. It is not that, in writing his later books, Herodotus discovered 'history' and rejected 'myth'; it is not that the storyteller of the previous half-century became the historian of the Persian wars. The same narrative skills are in play throughout; it is the quantity of information and the moral quality of what was remembered that change.

If we want to identify the characteristics that mark Herodotus' narrative as 'historical', the answer must lie in those aspects of his sense of the past identified fifty years ago by

R.G.Collingwood and developed more recently by Christian Meier:[25] that is to say, his grasp of the essential role of 'enquiry' and his perception of human experience not as the working-out of a divine 'will' but as the result of the interaction of multiple and contingent human purposes. Herodotus, we have seen, asks questions: he does not simply act as the repository of tradition, and he does not see events as the expression of a single will. The difference, in this latter respect, is immediately clear if we compare with Herodotean narrative the Old Testament narrative of, for example, the reigns of Saul and David in the first and second books of Kings. Two quotations will make the point. When Samuel in I Kings 12 summarizes the history of the Israelites since the Exodus, he does so as follows:

> It is the Lord that advanced Moses and Aaron and that brought your fathers up out of the land of Egypt. Now therefore stand still that I may reason with you before the Lord of all the righteous acts of the Lord, which he did to you and to your fathers. When Jacob was come into Egypt and your fathers cried unto the Lord, then the Lord sent Moses and Aaron, which brought your fathers out of Egypt and made them dwell in this place. And when they forgot the Lord their God, he sold them into the hands of Sisena, captain of the host of Hazor, and into the hands of the Philistines and into the hand of the king of Moab, and they fought against them. And they cried unto the Lord and said, we have sinned, because we have forsaken the Lord and have served Baalim and Astaroth, but now deliver us out of the hand of our enemies and we will serve thee. And the Lord sent Jerubbaal and Bedan and Jephthah and Samuel and delivered you out of the hand of your enemies on every side, and you dwelled safe. (I Kings 12.6–11)

The second quotation makes the contrast with Herodotus even more sharply: it is the account in Ezra of the decision of Cyrus the Great to authorize the return of the Jewish deportees from Babylon and the rebuilding of the temple in Jerusalem: 'Now in the first year of Cyrus king of Persia, that the world of the Lord by the mouth of Jeremiah might be fulfilled, the Lord stirred up the spirit of Cyrus, king of Persia, that he made a proclamation throughout all his kingdom and put it also in writing, saying; Thus saith Cyrus king of Persia: the Lord God of Heaven hath given me all the kingdoms of the earth; and he hath charged me to build him an house at Jerusalem, which is in Judah' (Ezra 1.1–2). Paradoxically, the Persian king might have recognized this account of his actions more readily than that of Herodotus: Dareius, on a brick stamp at Susa, says of himself, 'Of me is Ahura Mazda; of Ahura Mazda am I,' and attributes all his successes to the favour of the god.[26]

Herodotus' perception of the past has been called 'polycentric',[27] and it is a result of that perception that his narrative of the years from the middle of the sixth century to 479 BC is not a history of conflict between Greeks and non-Greeks seen exclusively from the point of view of the Greeks. It is rather one which presents events from a variety of points of view, even if narrated by a Greek for a Greek audience. That multiplicity of point of view and breadth of sympathy has been the cause of oscillation in judgments upon Herodotus in succeeding centuries, between, on the one hand, rejection of his work as biased and unpatriotic and, on the other, excited rediscoveries at times when suddenly expanded horizons of knowledge made it necessary for contemporaries to try to understand the world in less insular and parochial terms. The extreme of rejection is represented by a strange, tart and at times almost hysterical essay on Herodotus written by Plutarch probably towards the end of the first century AD. In this essay, 'On the Malignity of Herodotus', Herodotus is accused of being pro-barbarian and of preferring stories that belittle the achievements of the Greeks; in particular, he is accused of spiteful bias against Thebes and Corinth (Plutarch was a Boeotian) and of being ungenerous in his stories of Spartan hesitation and faint-heartedness in the struggle against Persia. Plutarch presents Herodotus as one who 'puts on a false show of good humour and frankness' which enables him to flatter, slander and malign without detection. It is an odd misreading but one that says a lot about how Herodotus struck a conventional Greek reader looking to history for praise of noble deeds and reinforcement of a sense of cultural superiority.

At other times and on other readers the impact of Herodotus' broad curiosity and open-minded readiness to understand the experience of others has been liberating and itself mind-opening. As Momigliano points out in his essay on Herodotus' place in the history of historiography, there have been periods in more than one culture when the sudden expansion of men's horizons by conquest or exploration has enforced a new perception of human experience. The result has been a disorientation of accepted modes of understanding which required a new model to make sense of the new data, and more than once Herodotus has supplied the model.[28] One such period in European culture was the discovery of the New World in the sixteenth century, when Spanish and Italian missionaries, ambassadors and explorers found themselves forced to depend on the collecting of oral tradition to supplement their own observations as travellers, and produced accounts of the history and culture of the peoples of America 'extraordinarily reminiscent of Herodotus both in style and method'. Recently, Oswyn Murray has shown that a similar reorientation of geographical and historical models took place in Arab culture in the period after the great conquests, particularly in the ninth and tenth centuries. In the ancient world itself Herodotus was both the beneficiary of and the model for an analogous attempt to make sense of an expanded world brought about, for the Greeks of the Hellenistic period, by the conquests of Alexander the Great. Those who commanded and accompanied Alexander's army and fleet used Herodotus as their guide to alien cultures and sought in their own experience for verification of Herodotus' statements. Thus Alexander's admiral Nearchus recorded that though he himself saw none of the gold-digging ants, 'smaller than dogs but larger than foxes', reported by Herodotus (3.102–5), nonetheless the skins of these creatures were brought into the Macedonian camp by native tribesmen and looked to him like panther skins (Nearchus fr. 8 Jacoby). Nearchus also used Herodotus' text as his model for the description of the geography of the river valleys of India and of the Arabian desert.[29] In the following two generations, other authors, both Greek and native, wrote accounts of the history and culture of the newly acquired territories of Egypt, India and the Near East for the enlightenment of their Greek ruling dynasties; these writers are everywhere indebted to Herodotus, in particular to his account of Egypt in Book Two, for their own portrayals of these countries as the source and cradle of civilization and as the model for an ideal, philosophical state – this in spite of the fact that in the same breath several of them explicitly reject Herodotus' account as the product of ignorance and naivety. A number of these writers, men such as Berossus, the Babylonian priest of Baal, and Manetho, the Egyptian high priest of Heliopolis, had access to the religious records of their own cultures, but Murray has shown that their model for making intelligible to their Greek masters and patrons this new world which an enforced enlargement of vision had opened up to them, remains the model of Herodotus, even when that model is mediated to them by others. The mediator is commonly the first Greek historian and ethnographer of the new territories, Hecataeus of Abdera, who wrote on the culture of Egypt within a decade or two of the Greek conquest. Hecataeus' work, elegantly structured on philosophical principles, has been described as 'the renewal of the Herodotean approach adapted to a more sophisticated age': the qualities that made Herodotus for all his alleged naivety, uniquely suitable for the role of model to the Hellenistic historians were precisely his largeness of vision, open-mindedness and comprehensiveness of imagination.

To these we should add, though it did not commend itself to some of his fellow Greeks, the range of his sympathy; the full significance of Herodotus' opening words ('in order that the human past may not be lost through the passage of time . . .') is only felt as the Herodotean narrative develops and unfolds. A brief look at two elements in his narrative will help to illustrate his breadth of sympathy: the ways in which women appear in the world of his *History*, and the range and quality of his sympathetic engagement with human suffering.

Women, it has been calculated, make 375 appearances in

Herodotus: this fact alone marks off Herodotus' world as strikingly different from that of Thucydides,[30] and from Greek historiography in general. Though it may be a rather one-sided and over-simple view of their role to say, as Carolyn Dewald does, that women in Herodotus display 'full partnership with men in establishing and maintaining social order' and that they 'are depicted working . . . to guarantee the stability of both family and culture',[31] nonetheless the very variety of their active interventions in events and the frequency with which the role played by women crucially determines the course of events, for both good and ill, is itself evidence of Herodotus' distinctive awareness that the world of history is not a single-sex world. Though sometimes he follows the conventions of a male-dominated world in which women are, for example, anonymous (Kandaules' wife, Demaratus' mother),[32] he shows himself remarkably sensitive to the full range of human experience as it is lived by women. Women in Herodotus are sometimes the powerless victims of male manipulations of the social order (Demaratus' mother and wife are both taken by their husbands from other men without reference to their own wishes: 6.62; 6.65.2), sometimes the innocent and unwitting causes of a catastrophic break of social continuity (Kanduales' wife; Astyages' daughter, who produces the son that kills her own father), sometimes the necessary, because sole, link that preserves continuity (Atossa, Cyrus' daughter, Cambyses' wife and then Xerxes' mother; Agariste, the granddaughter of Cleisthenes and mother of the 'Alcmeonid' Pericles: 6.131.1–2). Sometimes they betray their male blood-kindred out of loyalty to their husbands (the Spartan wives of Minyan husbands of 4.146.2–4); sometimes they assert the culture and traditions of their families of origin against that of their husbands (the Athenian women abducted to Lemnos by Pelasgians in 6.138).

But though there may be no single formula which covers the role of women in Herodotus, what is most striking throughout is what I would call the visibility of women in the world as Herodotus presents it, and their often paramount role in determining what happens; this is in stark contrast to the way in which the public world of political action

appears elsewhere in Greek literature. As Herodotus displays
the past, there would have been no tyranny in the history
of Corinth but for the active intervention of Labda, the lame,
unwanted daughter of the Bacchiad family, to protect her
infant son from murder by her own male kinsmen (5.92 b–d);
Artobazanes, the eldest son, not Xerxes, might have succeeded Dareius as king of Persia but for the 'complete power'
over Dareius' household held by Atossa, Xerxes' mother
(7.3.4); Sparta might, like Athens, have become fatally
involved in the Ionian revolt against Persia, if Cleomenes'
eight- or nine year-old daughter, Gorgo, had not intervened
to warn him against being tempted by the bribes offered by
Aristagoras (5.51). Though Herodotus' female characters may
be seen as ambiguous (for example, Artemisia the despot of
Halicarnassus in Books Seven and Eight),[33] or even as sinister
and vindictive (like Pheretime, the mother of Arkesilas of Cyrene and despot in his place: 4.162–7; 200–5), they take their
place with men in the historical world and the range of moral
judgment implicit in Herodotus' presentation of them is no
different from that which he offers by the same implication
on men. Tomyris, the queen of the Massagetae, as we have
seen, is as much a paradigmatic figure in marking the limits
of Persian expansion as the (unnamed) king of the Ethiopians
(pp. 103–5 above), though it is perhaps significant of what
female power means to Herodotus that whereas the Ethiopian
king represents an excess over the Persians in the direction
of culture and artifice, Tomyris outdoes them in violence and
bloodthirstiness, and her people are a people of the wild,
nomadic pastoralists and fishermen. The most striking case
of parallel male and female roles in Herodotus' narrative (one
of which Carolyn Dewald makes full use) is to be found in
his account of the origins of the Sauromatae, a tribe who
live across the Don from the Scythians (4.110–17). When a
group of Scythian men comes into contact with a marauding
band of Amazon women, the two groups gradually inter-
mingle until they form a joint encampment, but the Amazons
refuse to join an existing settlement which includes Scythian
women because they and the Scythian women have no common culture. They therefore persuade their men to form a

new tribe and migrate across the Don, but, as Herodotus stresses, the culture of the new tribe, the Sauromatae, retains the Amazon traditions of women hunting and fighting and their marriage rules require a woman to have killed a man in war before she can marry. The language of the tribe is Scythian, but a form of Scythian pidgin, because the Amazons had difficulties with the Scythian tongue and their mistakes have now been incorporated into the tribal language (the Scythian men, Herodotus reports, were quite unable to learn Amazon!). That story attests his open-eyed acknowledgment that human experience is multiform and that the role of women is culturally determined, not naturally 'given'. So too does his report that the women of the ordinary people in Lydia prostitute themselves to amass a dowry and give themselves away in marriage (1.93.4): both customs would have been unthinkable in any Greek community that Herodotus knew, but he reports them merely as an aside in his account of the building of the tomb of Croesus' father, Alyattes: the greater part of the building was done by these Lydian child prostitutes. His only comment is: 'Apart from the fact that they prostitute their female children, the Lydians have very much the same customs as the Greeks.'

The distinctive quality of Herodotus' perception of human experience is the tragic perception that it is always and everywhere vulnerable to time and chance and to the grim inevitabilities of existence. Of all the qualities that bear out Longinus' passing description of Herodotus as 'the most Homeric' of historians (13.3), it is perhaps this quality of sympathetic engagement with human suffering that is the most fundamental. Just as in the *Iliad* the moments that stick like burrs tenaciously in the memory are often the flashes of sympathetic engagement with the death of an otherwise unnoticed hero, so in Herodotus one recalls as essential to his vision of things the tiny moments which record, for example, that the Atarantes of the Libyan desert ('the only people that I know of to have no names') 'curse the sun as it rises and utter every obscenity at it, because it burns them and wears them down, their people and their land' (4.184.1–2), or that the Thracian tribe of the Trausoi differs from all the rest of the Thracian tribes only in that, when a child is born, its kinsmen gather round to lament and rehearse 'all the human sufferings of which it must full fill the measure' (the language once again involves an unmistakable Homeric echo) and again at its death 'rejoice and celebrate as they bury it in earth, listing the evils from which it has escaped' (5.4.1–2). One of the most arresting moments in Herodotus' narrative of Xerxes' invasion comes when the huge expeditionary force reaches the Hellespont at Abydos. Xerxes reviews[34] his troops and his fleet and watches a shiprace in the strait. 'As he watched all the strait hidden by his ships and all the beaches and the coastal plain of Abydos filled with his men, Xerxes declared himself to be under the protection of the gods; a moment later he burst into tears.' Herodotus continues:

His uncle Artabanus, the very man who at the outset had freely declared his mind in advising Xerxes not to invade Greece, on witnessing him burst into tears now asked Xerxes this: 'Sire, what you do now and what you did a moment ago are much at odds with each other: then you declared yourself under the protection of the gods; now you are in tears.' Xerxes said, 'Yes: it came home to me to be overcome with grief as I reckoned how short was human life: in a hundred years not one of all these thousands will be alive.' Artabanus replied: 'There are other things we suffer in life that are more pitiable than this. Even in so short a lifetime there is no man, since a man he is, not one of these here present nor of the rest of men, so favoured by the gods that it will not come to him to wish not once only, but again and again, that he were dead. The disasters of chance befall him; diseases bewilder and confuse him; and they make life, short as it is, seem long. This is how death comes to be a man's most desired refuge from the distress of living; even in giving us a taste of the sweetness of life god is found a jealous giver.' Xerxes replied: 'Let us talk no more, Artabanus, about human life: it is as you describe it. Let us not remind ourselves of evils when we have good things in hand. ...' (7.45–7)

The whole scene takes your breath away. Here is the great enemy, the man whom Herodotus' Themistocles is to describe as 'unholy and wicked' (8.109.3), who has just had the Hellespont lashed with three hundred lashes because it dared to challenge its 'master' ('Xerxes the king will cross you, whether you wish it or not' 7.35), presented as the paradigm of a human being suddenly overtaken by the perception of the universal vulnerability of men. It is a fleeting realization which only for a moment holds up the unstoppable forward momentum of the vast expedition; it has none of the finality of the dialogue between Priam and Achilles in the last book of the *Iliad*. But it is unforgettable nonetheless because, like that dialogue, it gives expression to a universal truth which overrides enmity and cultural difference: in their openness to chance all men are one. That is not 'the meaning of events' in Herodotus' *History*, but it is the backdrop against which events are understood to have meaning.

Yet, even in saying this, Herodotus' achievement is distorted. For the most lasting of all impressions that one takes away from a reading of his narrative is exhilaration. It comes from the sense one has of Herodotus' inexhaustible curiosity and vitality. He responds with ever-present delight and admiration to the 'astonishing' variety of human achievement and invention in a world which he acknowledges as tragic; he makes you laugh, not by presenting experience as comic, but by showing it as constantly surprising and stimulating; he makes you glad to have read him by showing men responding to suffering and disaster with energy and ingenuity, resilient and undefeated.

Notes

EPIGRAPH

Walter Benjamin, 'The Storyteller', *Illuminations* (London, 1973), 83.

1. THE WORLD OF HERODOTUS

1 R.Meiggs and D.M.Lewis, *A Selection of Greek Historical Inscriptions to the End of the Fifth Century BC* (Oxford, 1969), no. 12.

2 For example, 3.140; 8.86.3. The phrase 'great gratitude shall be stored up for you in the King's house' is echoed in Thucydides' account of Xerxes' letter to the Spartan general Pausanias (Thucydides 1.129).

3 See R.G.Kent, *Old Persian: Grammar, Texts, Lexikon*, 2nd edn (New Haven, 1953), 107–8, 116–35. The inscription is illustrated on the frontispiece.

4 J.M.Cook, *The Persian Empire* (London, 1983), 71–2.

5 For the journey time and the 'royal road' that connected Susa to the Aegean coast, see Herodotus 5.50–4.

6 The Greek text is given in H.Diels, *Die Fragmente der Vorsokratiker*, 6th edn, revised W.Kranz (Berlin, 1951): Xenophanes in no. 21 in Diels' collection and the quotation is from fragment B22. Other references to this collection are identified by the letters DK after the fragment number.

7 G.E.Bean and J.M.Cook, 'The Halicarnassus Peninsula', *Annual of the British School at Athens* 50 (1955), 96; S.Hornblower, *Mausolus* (Oxford, 1982), 4–31, gives an account of the geography and history of Caria down to the period of Herodotus' death.

8 S.Hornblower, *The Greek World* 479–323 BC (London

and New York, 1985), 63 and 66, quoting A. Cowley, *Aramaic Papyri* (Oxford, 1923).

9 First cousin seems the more likely: see the arguments adduced by V. J. Matthews, *Panyassis of Halikarnassos* (Leiden, 1974), 10–12. The inscription is no. 32 in Meiggs and Lewis (note 1 above).

10 Edward Hussey, *The Presocratics* (London, 1972), 7.

11 For Thales' interest in the question, see Thales 11.A.1 DK, and for fifth-century speculation, Anaxagoras 59.A.91 DK, Diogenes of Apollonia 64.A.18 DK and generally Aetius 4.11ff.

12 G. E. R. Lloyd, *Magic, Reason and Experience* (Cambridge, 1979), 24ff., 69ff.

13 A. Momigliano, *Alien Wisdom: The Limits of Hellenization* (Cambridge, 1975), 56–60, 74.

14 Democritus 68.A.33 DK; Euripides fr. 910 Nauck (*Tragicorum Graecorum Fragmenta*, 2nd edn, Berlin, 1889); G. E. M. de Ste. Croix, *Greece and Rome*, n.s. 24 (1977), 130–2.

15 On the development of the meaning of the word *historie* towards the technical sense 'history' and for a good discussion of the nature of Herodotus' activity as 'enquirer' and writer, see S. Hornblower, *Thucydides* (London, 1987), 8–25.

16 Herodotus' accounts of his travels and his pursuit of eyewitness evidence have been called into question by Detlev Fehling in his book *Die Quellenangaben bei Herodot* (Berlin and New York, 1971). Fehling draws attention to Herodotus' invariable citation of 'on the spot' evidence for his assertions (the 'principle of the nearest witness') and to the inherent improbability of many of his reported testimonies. He argues that 'no one at Babylon ever knew anything of the tower of Babel' (12) and that claims by Herodotus to have obtained his evidence from local eyewitnesses are fictions: Herodotus is a storyteller whose consistent claims to have 'been there' himself put him in the tradition of Baron von Münchhausen, though rather before his time. It follows that Herodotus' recurring anxiety to distinguish between first-hand evidence and

remoter chains of testimony, and between information gained from different traditions, is systematic lying to make his stories seem more authentic. This is not the place for a detailed counter-argument and in any case judgment here is perhaps inevitably subjective to a greater degree than elsewhere: for my part, I find the resulting picture of Herodotus impossible to believe. See further the helpful discussion of Fehling's arguments by Carolyn Dewald (*Arethusa* 20, 1987, 26–32) and note also Oswyn Murray's comment that Fehling's argument 'implies a proto-Herodotus before Herodotus' (Heleen Sancisi-Weerdenburg and Amélie Kuhrt, eds., *Achaemenid History II: The Greek Sources*, Leiden, 1987, 101, n. 12).

17 Aristophanes, *Acharnians*, 523–9. It has recently been argued (for example by D.M.MacDowell, *Greece and Rome*, n.s. 30, 1983, 151–3) that the resemblance is mere coincidence and the parody (if there is any) of Euripides' play *Telephus*. But against this see D.Sansone, *Illinois Classical Studies* 10 (1985), 1–9.

18 See above all, Charles Fornara, *Herodotus: An Interpretative Essay* (Oxford, 1971), 37–91. For further discussion of Herodotus' purpose in writing, see below, pp. 116–20.

19 Thucydides' famous sentence about his own work as a 'possession for all time' (1.22.4) ends with the words, 'it has been composed *to be heard*'. Stewart Flory ('Who read Herodotus' *Histories*?', *American Journal of Philology* 101, 1980, 12–28) has argued that the length and coherence of Herodotus' text make it impossible that he intended it to be recited either as a whole or in excerpt, and that therefore Herodotus' audience was 'a relatively small and elite audience of readers'. But we are dealing with a culture with a quite different experience from our own of extended performance (of Homer's *Iliad* and *Odyssey*, for example), and it is dangerous to offer arguments of probability based on our own experience in such things.

2. 'ENQUIRY' AND 'SOCIAL MEMORY'

1 Nigel Bailey, *The Innocent Anthropologist* (Harmondsworth, 1986), 83.

2 Thebes, along with most of the other Greek cities of Boeo-
tia, had 'medized', that is, accepted the suzerainty of Persia, and were now fighting with the Persians against their
fellow Greeks. Hence the banquet given for the Persian
high command.

3 J.M.Cook, *The Persian Empire* (Chapter 1, n. 4 above),
49; A.B.Lloyd, 'Herodotus on Cambyses: some thoughts
on recent work' (Amélie Kuhrt and Heleen Sancisi-Weerdenburg, eds., *Achaemenid History III: Method and
Theory*, Leiden, 1988, 55–66).

4 So D.M.Lewis, 'Persians in Herodotus' (*The Greek His-
torians: Literature and History: Essays presented to
A.E.Raubitschek*, Stanford, 1986, 107–8); id., *Sparta and
Persia* (Leiden, 1977), 12–15.

5 Barley, *The Innocent Anthropologist* (Harmondsworth,
1986), 54ff.

6 On Herodotus' understanding of Persian religion, see
J.M.Cook, *The Persian Empire* (Chapter 1, n. 4 above),
150–55; R.C.Zaehner, *The Dawn and Twilight of Zoroas-
trianism* (London, 1961), 154–67; most recently,
M.Boyce, 'The religion of Cyrus the Great' (Kuhrt and
Sancisi-Weerdenburg, eds., *Achaemenid History III*, 15–
31, esp. 22–3).

7 Jan Vansina, *Oral Tradition* (Harmondsworth, 1973);
Oral Tradition as History (London, 1985); Ruth Finnegan, *Oral Literature in Africa* (London, 1970); 'A note
on Oral Tradition and Historical Evidence' (*History and
Theory* 9 (1970), 195–201); J.Goody and I.Watt, 'The
Consequences of Literacy' in *Literacy in Traditional Societies*, ed. J.Goody (Cambridge, 1968), 27–68; J.Goody,
The Domestication of the Savage Mind (Cambridge,
1977); Mabel Lang, 'Herodotus: Oral History with a Difference' (*Proceedings of the American Philosophical
Society* 128, 1984, 93–103); J.A.S.Evans, 'Oral tradition
in Herodotus' (*Canadian Oral History Association Journal* 4 (1980), 8–16. There is a good, though brief, discussion of Herodotus' use of oral tradition in the same
author's *Herodotus* (Boston, 1982), 146–53. Oswyn
Murray's essay 'Herodotus and Oral History' (Kuhrt and

Sancisi-Weerdenburg, eds., *Archaemenid History II*, 93–115) is now the best and most sophisticated discussion of the question, though his attempt to distinguish between Greek and Persian traditions is open to objection. The influential essay by Moses Finley, 'Myth, meaning and history' (*History and Theory* 4, 1965, 281–302, reprinted in *The Use and Abuse of History*, London, 1975, 11–33) considers the issues involved too much in the abstract and is hence over-sceptical.

8 See, for example, D.Nugent, *Critique of Anthropology* 15 (1985), 71–86; E.P.Thompson, 'Folklore, Anthroplogy and History' (*Studies in Labour History* pamphlet, 1978–9); Anna Collard, 'Anthropology and History: An Investigation into the Question of 'Social Memory' in the Greek Context' (unpublished paper).

9 On the motif-structure of the Gyges story, see *Journal of Hellenic Studies* 100 (1980), 52–5.

10 R.Drews, 'Sargon, Cyrus and Mesopotamian Folk-History', *Journal of Near Eastern Studies* 33 (1974), 387–93; J.M.Cook, *The Persian Empire* (Chapter 1, n. 4 above), 26–7.

11 W.Aly, *Volksmärchen, Sage und Novelle bei Herodot und seine Zeitgenossen* (Göttingen, 1921), 196–7.

12 The naming of a rich Athenian after the Lydian king is perhaps evidence of the existence already of ritualized friendship (*xenia*) between the two families: so G.Herman, *Ritualized Friendship and the Greek City* (Cambridge, 1987), 19–21.

13 On Herodotus' debt to the painting in the Stoa Poikile, see most recently E.D.Francis and M.Vickers, *Annual of the British School at Athens* 80 (1985), 109–13.

14 The author and journalist Arthur Machen claimed that the legend had its origin in a piece of fiction of his own called *The Bowmen*, but second-hand reports from eyewitnesses of the intervention of St George in the fighting round the Mons salient on 24 August 1914 appeared already in the August 1915 issue of *The Occult Review*: see A. Machen, *The Bowmen and Other Legends of the War* (London, 1915), 7–21, 81–3.

15 A.Collard (n. 6 above).
16 S.Hornblower, *The Greek World* 479–323 BC (Chapter 1, n. 7 above), 15–17.
17 The most thorough and most convincing treatment of Herodotus' grasp of chronology is Herman Strasburger's paper 'Herodots Zeitrechnung', reprinted in his *Studien zur Alten Geschichte* (Hildesheim and New York, 1982), vol. II, 627–75.
18 J.Goody, *The Domestication of the Savage Mind* (n. 5 above).
19 J. Redfield, 'Commentary' in *Arethusa* 20 (1987), 252.

3. THE LOGIC OF NARRATIVE

1 Marcel Mauss, *Essai sur le don* (1925; reprinted in *Sociologie et Anthropologie*, Paris, 1966; translated as *The Gift*, tr. Ian Cunnison, London, 1966).
2 I hope to discuss the significance of giving, taking and giving back in Herodotus in my forthcoming J.L.Myres Memorial Lecture (Oxford, 1989).
3 G.Herman (Chapter 2, n. 10 above).
4 E.E.Evans-Pritchard, *The Nuer* (Oxford, 1940), 108.
5 'Supplication' in ancient Greek culture is a complex of ritual gestures involving physical contact combined with acts of self-abasement which creates ties of solidarity and obligation between strangers or even on occasion between enemies: I have discussed the ritual and its symbolism in *Journal of Hellenic Studies* 93 (1973), 74–103.
6 Evans-Pritchard, *The Nuer* (n. 4 above), 144.
7 Hayden White, 'The Value of Narrativity in the Representation of Reality', in W.J.T.Mitchell, ed., *On Narrative* (Chicago and London, 1981), 1–23: White's discussion of the Saint Gall chronicles is on pp. 7–11. See also his essay 'The Question of Narrative in Contemporary Historical Theory' (*History and Theory* 23, 1984, 1–33).
8 See the full and critical treatment of the question by Stephanie West, 'Herodotus' Epigraphical Interests', in *Classical Quarterly* n.s. 35 (1985), 278–305.
9 Gregory Nagy, 'Herodotus the *Logios*', in *Arethusa* 20

(1987), 175–84; see also his *The Best of the Achaeans* (Baltimore and London, 1979), 15–17, 26–41, 94–103.

10 The story of Thrasyboulos' deception of Alyattes by creating the appearance of infinite resources looks like another recurring folk-motif: cf. Thucydides' story of a strikingly similar deception, practised on Athens by the inhabitants of Segesta in Sicily (Thucydides 6.46.1–4). K.J.Dover notes the inherent improbability of Thucydides' report: see his note in Gomme, Andrewes and Dover, *Historical Commentary on Thucydides* (Oxford, 1970), vol. IV, 312–3.

11 See J.D.Denniston, *Greek Prose Style* (Oxford, 1952), 5–8.

12 This is not because simile and metaphor are alien to historical writing (because associated with epic): for a later example of their frequent use, see Thomas Wiedemann, 'Between Beasts and Men:Barbarians in Ammianus Marcellinus', in Moxon, Smart and Woodman, eds., *Past Perspectives: Studies in Greek and Latin Historical Writing* (Cambridge, 1986), 196–201.

13 For the connection between figurative action and the language of oracles, see my essay 'On Making Sense of Greek Religion', in Easterling and Muir, eds., *Greek Religion and Society* (Cambridge, 1985), 22–4.

14 Momigliano, *Alien Wisdom* (Chapter 1, n. 12 above), 25: 'Polybius lacks the sense of surprise. He is the prototype of the historian who never marvels, just as Herodotus is the prototype of the historian who always marvels.'

15 So, rightly, Hugh Lloyd-Jones, *The Justice of Zeus* (Berkeley, Los Angeles and London, 1971), 65–6. See also James Redfield, *Classical Philology* 80 (1985), 109–114; *Arethusa* 20 (1987), 252.

4. WHY THINGS HAPPEN

1 Mabel Lang, *Herodotean Narrative and Discourse* (Cambridge, Mass. and London, 1984), 12, 79.

2 J.de Romilly, 'La vengeance comme explication historique dans l'oeuvre d'Hérodote' (*Revue des Etudes Grecques* 84, 1971, 314–37): the quotations are from pp. 318 and 320.

3 W.G.Forrest, 'Motivation in Herodotus: The Case of the Ionian Revolt' (*International History Review* 1, 1979, 311–22). It is instructive to compare Herodotus' account of the Samian tyranny and its downfall with that of a modern historian: see Graham Shipley, *A History of Samos* (Oxford, 1987), 69–109.

4 So, rightly, G.E.M.de Ste. Croix, *Greece and Rome* n.s. 24 (1977), 144–5.

5 It is slightly disconcerting to recognise in the alternations of day and night and the corresponding reversals in decision-making in Herodotus' narrative the nearest analogue to the double decision-making process (once drunk, then sober – or vice versa) reported of the Persians by Herodotus in 1.133.3–4.

6 Ieuan Lewis, *Social Anthropology in Perspective* (Harmondsworth, 1976), 72–7, summarising the research of E.E.Evans-Pritchard, *Witchcraft, Oracles and Magic among the Azande* (Oxford, 1937).

7 Notice, for example, the logic of Agamemnon's argument in his so-called speech of 'apology' in *Iliad* 19: he argues that he was 'not responsible' for the insult given to Achilles, but that 'Zeus and Fate and the Fury that walks in mist' implanted 'delusion' in his mind. He tells a story of how even Zeus was once 'deluded' and made a mistaken decision: he then continues 'But *since* I was deluded and Zeus took my wits from me, I am ready to . . . give recompense beyond calculation' (*Iliad* 19.86–138). There is no sense in which the supernatural explanation leads to a disavowal of practical responsibility.

8 Mary Douglas, *Evans-Pritchard* (Fontana Modern Masters: London, 1980), 51.

9 A good example of 'luxuriant multiplicity' and of supernatural explanation combined with human accountability is the story of the death of Croesus' son, Atys. The story is introduced by the comment: 'The anger of a god now overtook Croesus . . . because he thought himself the most blessed of men,' but it ends with the accidental killer, Adrastus, himself taking his own life as an act of requital, because he acknowledges that he is 'the most ill-fated of

men' (compare 1.34 with 1.45.2–3).

10 Mabel Lang, *Herodotean Narrative and Discourse* (n. 1 above), 64.

11 See Richard Rutherford, 'Tragic Form and Feeling in the *Iliad*' (*Journal of Hellenic Studies* 102, 1982, 145–60), and my essay 'Homeric Epic and the Tragic Moment' in *Aspects of the Epic* (eds. Winnifrith, Murray and Gransden, London, 1983), 32–45.

12 It *is* argued: see below, pp. 79–81.

13 See H.-P. Stahl, 'Learning Through Suffering?' (*Yale Classical Studies* 24, 1975, 1–36) for some reservations as to the wisdom of the fallen Croesus. The motif of the 'tragic warner' or 'wise adviser' and his/her advice is well analysed by H. Bischoff in his dissertation *Der Warner bei Herodot* (Marburg, 1932), and by Richmond Lattimore in his essay 'The Wise Adviser in Herodotus' (*Classical Philology* 34, 1939, 24–35).

14 C. Fornara, *Herodotus* (Chapter 1, n. 16 above), 77–8. Fornara speaks also of Herodotus' acceptance of 'inevitable laws of history' and of his 'conception of historical inevitability'.

15 Mabel Lang (n. 1 above), 62.

16 See Easterling and Muir, eds., *Greek Religion and Society* (Chapter 3, n. 12 above), 11–14.

17 Walter Benjamin, *Illuminations* (London, 1973), 108.

18 Roy Schafer in W. J. T. Mitchell (ed.), *On Narrative* (Chapter 3, n. 6 above), 27 n. 2.

19 Evans-Pritchard, *The Nuer* (Chapter 3, n. 4 above), 171–2.

20 For examples, see Antiphon 4b.1; Lysias 4.11; Isocrates 20.1; Demosthenes 47.7–8, 15, 35, 39–40, 47; 23.50.

5. MAPPING OTHER WORLDS

1 Evans-Pritchard, *The Nuer* (Chapter 3, n. 4 above), 108, 198–200. The tree under which mankind came into being was still standing in Western Nuerland in the 1930s.

2 For a discussion of Herodotus' story, see A. B. Lloyd, *Journal of Egyptian Archaeology* 63 (1977), 142–55. Lloyd concludes, on what seem to me not quite adequate grounds, against the truth of the story Herodotus records.

3 Ever since Hermann Diels' article of 1887, the idea has been widespread that Herodotus silently draws on the work of Hecataeus and presents it as the result of his own enquiries. But the surviving quotations from Hecataeus' (lost) work collected by Felix Jacoby strongly suggest that the whole scale and range of his *narrative* interest in the traditions he collected was very slight and that it could not possibly have been reproduced to yield what Herodotus gives us, in spite of such arguments to the contrary as those of W.A.Heidel in his essay 'Hecataeus and the Egyptian Priests in Herodotus, Book II' (Boston, 1935). Hecataeus' main achievement was as a voyager and geographer (where his knowledge of the Mediterranean coastline is detailed and impressive); his interest in narrative was perhaps secondary.

4 On Aristeas, his poems and his travels, see J.D.P.Bolton, *Aristeas of Proconnesus* (Oxford, 1962), esp. 1–19, 74–141; Jan Bremmer, *The Early Greek Concept of the Soul* (Princeton, 1983), 25–38, 43–53.

5 For the Delian begging procession and its mythical and ritual connections, see Walter Burkert, *Structure and History in Greek Mythology and Ritual* (Berkeley, Los Angeles and London, 1979), Chap. 6, esp. 134–5 and 208 n. 8.

6 The best discussion of Herodotus' cultural geography is to be found in François Hartog's book *Le miroir d'Hérodote: essai sur la représentation de l'autre* (Paris, 1980). Hartog's analysis of Herodotus' conceptualization of space is subtle and penetrating, especially his account of the systematic opposition between Scythia and Egypt, but it tends to deny altogether the contribution of observation, whether derived from others or first-hand. The account in the text represents, I hope, a more balanced estimate of the different factors at work in Herodotus' thinking. See also G.E.R.Lloyd, *Polarity and Analogy* (Cambridge, 1966), 341–5.

7 See J.M.Cook, *The Persian Empire* (Chapter 1, n. 4 above), 77–82; D.M.Lewis, 'Persians in Herodotus' (*The Greek Historians*, Chapter 2, n. 2 above), esp. 102–4.

8 James Redfield, 'Herodotus the Tourist', *Classical Philology* 80 (1985), 103–4, 105–10. Redfield's essay is the best account known to me of the character of Herodotus' thinking about culture and of the factors that determined his cultural perceptions.

9 As has been pointed out more than once, Herodotus' perception of parallels between culture and environment is not peculiar to him: it recurs in an even more thoroughgoing and intricate form in the fifth-century 'Hippocratic' work *Airs, Water, Places* (*Hippocratic Writings*, ed. G.E.R.Lloyd, Harmondsworth, 1978, 148–69).

10 As Redfield remarks, 'Herodotus does not get inside the Persian mind enough to see that their policies [or religious behaviour] were from their point of view, thoughtful' ('Herodotus the Tourist', n. 7 above, 117).

11 How and Wells, *A Commentary on Herodotus* (Oxford, 1912), vol. I, 48–9.

12 The identification of Hestia as a principal goddess of the nomadic Scythians is highly surprising in view of the symbolic connection between Hestia and the fixity and permanence of the household, and the opposition between flocks and herds and fixed property, for which see J.-P.Vernant's essay 'Hestia-Hermes' in *Mythe et Pensée chez les Grecs* (Paris, 1971), vol. I, 124–70; Hartog, *Le miroir d'Hérodote* (n. 5 above), 135–41.

13 For the royal burials and hemp-smoke-inhaling of the Scyths, see T.Sulimirski in *The Cambridge History of Iran* (Cambridge, 1985), vol. II, 158–9, 170–3, 181–2, and the finds from the frozen tombs of the Altai (*Frozen Tombs: the culture and art of the ancient tribes of Siberia*, British Museum, London, 1978, 22–4, 47–8).

14 On purification by fumigation in Greek culture, see Robert Parker, *Miasma: Pollution and Purification in Early Greek Religion* (Oxford, 1983), 227–8.

15 For a systematic treatment of polarity as a matrix for organizing experience, see Part 1 of G.E.R.Lloyd, *Polarity and Analogy* (n. 5 above); on inversion as a form of cultural marginalisation, see Thomas Wiedemann, 'Between Men and Beasts' (Chapter 3, n. 11 above), 189–93.

16 I have developed a similar argument in attempting to describe the coherence of ancient Greek religion in my essay 'On Making Sense of Greek Religion' (Chapter 3, n. 12 above).

6. READING HERODOTUS

1 Hence perhaps his frequently expressed disbelief in the existence of Ocean, the stream that bounds the earth in much mythical geography.

2 Carolyn Dewald, 'Narrative Surface and Authorial Voice in Herodotus' *Histories*' in *Arethusa* 20 (1987), 147–70: the quotation is from p. 167.

3 Thucydides 1.21–2. So too for Aristotle, Herodotus is 'the storyteller' in a pejorative sense (Aristotle, *De generatione animalium* 3.5, 756b 6; fr. 248 Rose), as also for the Hellenistic historian Hellanicus of Abdera, quoted by Diodorus Siculus 1.69.7.

4 Momigliano, 'The Place of Herodotus in the History of Historiography', *History* 43 (1958), reprinted in his *Studies in Historiography* (London, 1966, 127–42).

5 A.W.Gomme, 'Herodotos and Marathon', *Phoenix* 6 (1952), 77–83, reprinted in his *More Essays in Greek History and Literature* (Oxford, 1962), 29–37 (my italics).

6 D.M.Lewis, 'Persians in Herodotus' (Chapter 2, n. 2 above), 105–6.

7 Gomme (n. 5 above), p. 31 of the reprinted text.

8 Momigliano, 'Some Observations on the Causes of War in Ancient Historiography', *Proceedings of the Second International Congress of Classical Studies* (Copenhagen, 1958), vol. I, 199–211, reprinted in *Studies in Historiography* (n. 4 above), 112–26: the quotations are from pp. 120 and 124 of the reprinted text.

9 Henry Immerwahr, *Form and Meaning in Herodotus* (Cleveland, 1956), 203. Immerwahr's book is one of the best discussions of Herodotus' thinking in relation to his narrative; see also his essays 'Historical action in Herodotus' (*Transactions of the American Philological Association* 85, 1954, 14–45), and 'Aspects of Historical Causation in Herodotus' (TAPA 87, 1956, 241–80).

10 J.de Romilly (Chapter 4, n. 2 above), 320.

11 The point was convincingly demonstrated against earlier interpretations of Herodotus' view of Periclean Athens by Herman Strasburger in his essay 'Herodot und das Perikleischen Athen', *Historia* 4, 1955, 1–25, reprinted in his *Studien zur Alten Geschichte*, Wiesbaden, 1982, vol. II, 592–626).

12 Aristotle, *Rhetoric* 3.10 1411a 1–4.

13 Fornara (Chapter 1, n. 16 above), 90.

14 Kurt A.Raaflaub, 'Herodotus, Political Thought and the Meaning of History', *Arethusa* 20 (1987), 221–48.

15 The parallelism is acutely analysed by Tilman Krischer, 'Herodots Prooimion' (*Hermes* 93, 1965, 159–67). Krischer distinguishes between the Homeric overtones of the second half of Herodotus' opening sentence and the way the opening is linked to the following narrative, and the more 'modern' implications of 'enquiry' contained, as he sees it, in the first half.

16 Nagy, 'Herodotus the *Logios*' (Chapter 3, n. 8 above).

17 For Pindar, see especially *Nemean* 6.28–30, 45–7; *Pythian* 1.92–4.

18 See, for example, the argument presented by Kurt von Fritz in his *Die griechische Geschichtsschreibung* (Berlin, 1967), vol. I, 208–79, 442–75.

19 The time lapse is usually given as the fifth generation through misunderstanding of the Greek convention of counting both first and last in ordinal numeration (so that 'every other year' becomes 'every third year'): the evidence for four generations in this case is given in the ancestry of Croesus as recorded in 1.15–16 and 26.

20 Evans-Pritchard, *Witchcraft, Oracles and Magic among the Azande* (Chapter 4, n. 6 above), 12.

21 So already Hugh Lloyd-Jones, *The Justice of Zeus* (Chapter 3, n. 14 above), 62–3.

22 D.M.Lewis, 'Persians in Herodotus' (Chapter 2, n. 2 above), 113–6; A.R.Burn, *Persia and the Greeks* (London, 1962), 322–5.

23 J.M.Cook, *The Persian Empire* (Chapter 1, n. 4 above), 18–20. There are already gaps in Herodotus' knowledge

of Dareius' high officials: see D.M.Lewis, 'Datis the Mede' (*Journal of Hellenic Studies* 100, 1980, 194–5).

24 For example, Croesus' generosity to Alcmaeon, the ancestor of the Alcmaeonid family, as recorded by Herodotus (6.125). The story may have been one told at Athens against Alcmaeon and his family: Alcmaeon is made to seem ludicrous as well as grasping. But there is no suggestion that *Croesus* is being shown unfavourably, and the likelihood that Herodotus or his tradition has confused Croesus with his father Alyattes only strengthens the significance of the story for Croesus' reputation at Athens. See further J.K.Davies, *Athenian Propertied Families* (Oxford, 1971), 369–71.

25 R.G.Collingwood, *The Idea of History* (Oxford, 1946), 9–20; Christian Meier, 'The Origins of History in Ancient Greece', *Arethusa* 20 (1987), 41–57.

26 J.M.Cook, *The Persian Empire* (Chapter 1, n. 4 above), 197.

27 The term is Sally Humphreys' alternative (and preferable) formulation of Christian Meier's word 'multi-subjectivity' for the same tendency in Herodotus' thinking: *Arethusa* 20 (1987), 219.

28 Momigliano (n. 4 above), 136–40.

29 Oswyn Murray, 'Herodotus and Hellenistic Culture' (*Classical Quarterly* n.s. 22, 1972, 200–13).

30 Thomas Wiedemann, 'Women in Thucydides' (*Greece and Rome* n.s. 30, 1983, 163–70).

31 Carolyn Dewald, 'Women and Culture in Herodotus' *Histories*', in Helene Foley, ed., *Reflections of Women in Antiquity* (New York, London, Paris, 1981), 91–125: the quotations are from pp. 92 and 97.

32 On naming and anonymity of women in Greek literature, see *Journal of Hellenic Studies* 100 (1980), 45; D.Schaps, *Classical Quarterly* n.s. 27 (1977), 323–30.

33 On Artemisia, see Carolyn Dewald (n. 31 above), 109–10 and 125 (for the 'Halicarnassian' aspect of her inversion of gender roles).

34 David Konstam has drawn attention to the Persian obsession with reviewing and counting in Herodotus' nar-

rative (*Arethusa* 20, 1987, 63–6, 72–3); his examples include 7.59.2–3, 60.2–3, 81, 100.1, 101–4, and 8.24–5 as well as 7.45. The sequence 'joy, tears, understanding' in Herodotus is traced by Stewart Flory in his essay 'Laughter, Tears and Wisdom in Herodotus' (*American Journal of Philology* 99, 1978, 145–53).

A Note on
Further Reading

The standard Greek text of Herodotus is by K. Hude in the Oxford Classical Texts series. The most readable and the most enjoyable (but not in detail the most reliable) English translation is by Aubrey de Selincourt (Penguin Classics; 2nd edn. Harmondsworth, 1972: the second edition has a useful introduction by A.R.Burn); a more accurate but less exhilarating version is that by George Rawlinson, once available in the Everyman series but now out of print. The recent translation by David Grene (Chicago, 1987) sets out to capture the 'peculiar quality' of Herodotus' language: the result is a quirky but affectionate version.

The best brief introductions to the achievement of Herodotus are probably the article by G.E.M. de Ste Croix (*Greece and Rome* n.s. 24 1977, 130–48) and the introduction by W.G.Forrest to the abridged edition of George Rawlinson's translation of Herodotus in the Great Histories series (ed. H.R.Trevor-Roper, New English Library, 1963). There are good, longer introductions by John Hart (*Herodotus and Greek History*, London and Canberra, 1982) and by J.A.S. Evans (*Herodotus*: Twayne's World Authors, Boston, 1982). An earlier but still classic general treatment of Herodotus is J.L.Myres, *Herodotus, Father of History* (Oxford, 1953). Modern discussion of Herodotus goes back to Felix Jacoby's classic, book-length article of 1913, first published in the second Supplementband to Pauly-Wissowa, *Realencyclopädie des Altertumswissenschaft* (cols. 205–520) and reprinted in his *Griechische Historiker* (Stuttgart, 1956), pp. 7–164 but never translated into English.

The commentary by W.W.How and J.Wells (on the Greek text: Oxford, 1912, 2 vols.) is now much outdated by subsequent research and excavation, but it remains useful and has not been replaced. The detailed commentary on Book 2 by

A.B.Lloyd (3 vols., Leiden, 1975–88) contains much that is relevant to Herodotus' text as a whole. Enoch Powell's *Lexicon to Herodotus* (Cambridge, 1939, reprinted Hildesheim, 1960), an index to Herodotus' Greek text as well as a lexicon, is an indispensable tool in any research into Herodotus.

The world into which Herodotus was born, dominated by the power of Persia, is now well described in J.M.Cook's *The Persian Empire* (London, 1983) and in Volume 2 of the *Cambridge History of Iran* (Cambridge, 1985), which covers the nomadic Scythians as well as the more settled populations of Asia Minor and gives access to the work of Russian archaeologists on Scythian sites north of the Black Sea. The history of the period covered by Herodotus' enquiries is the subject of two books by A.R.Burn (*The Lyric Age of Greece*, London, 1967 and *Persia and the Greeks*, 2nd edition, London, 1984, with an important postscript by D.M.Lewis); also of two recent re-examinations, Oswyn Murray's *Early Greece* (Brighton, 1980) and Anthony Snodgrass' *Archaic Greece* (London, 1980): a comparison of the two last will show how much the history of the period is still a matter of debate and open to re-interpretation in terms of new models and perceptions of archaic Greek society and economy, as well as new evidence from excavation and from non-Greek sources. There are good examples of the debate on sources and perceptions in the *Proceedings* of the 1984 and 1985 Achaemenid History Workshops, held in Groningen and London respectively (Kuhrt and Sancisi-Weerdenburg, eds., Leiden, 1987 and 1988).

The debate on Herodotus' sources and the extent to which his own account of his enquiries is to be believed was given a new lease of life by Detlev Fehling's *Die Quellenangaben bei Herodot* (Berlin and New York, 1971); see also the articles of O.K.Armayor, 'Did Herodotus ever go to the Black Sea?' (*Harvard Studies in Classical Philology* 82, 1978, 45–62); 'Sesostris and Herodotus' autopsy of Thrace, Colchis, Inland Asia Minor and the Levant' (*Harvard Studies* 84, 1980, 51–74); 'Did Herodotus ever go to Egypt?' (*Journal of the American Research Center in Egypt* 15, 1980, 59–71) and the same author's *Herodotus' autopsy of the Fayoum* (Amsterdam, 1985). There has been no adequate, detailed reply to Fehling's argument, but see Chapter 1, note 15 above. Any adequate reply would have to start from the concepts of oral tradition and social memory developed over the last two decades by anthropologists and historians: see Chapter 2, notes 5 and 6 above. The growing interest in such questions is well exemplified by two recent articles: Alan Griffiths' 'Democedes of Croton: a Greek doctor at Darius' court' (Kuhrt and Sancisi–Weerdenburg, eds., *Achaemenid History II: the Greek Sources*, Leiden, 1987, 37–51) and Christiane Sourvinou-Inwood's '"Myth" and History: on Herodotus III 48 and 50–53' (*Opuscula Atheniensia* 17, 1988, 167–82).

The date of 'publication' of Herodotus' work is an issue which raises problems both about the manner of its diffusion and about the critical question of how much was known to whom when and where: J. A. S. Evans, for example, argues that the 'Persian debate' of 3.80ff. and the story of Dareius' accession of which it is part were 'published . . . in some way or other' before the rest of the work, probably in the 440s BC and were known in Athens at this time (*Quaderni Urbinati* n.s. 7, 1981, 79–84). The latest date offered by scholars would have the work as we have it in circulation not long before 414 BC: so C. W. Fornara, *Journal of Hellenic Studies* 91, 1971, 25–34. Fornara's arguments were criticized and rejected by J. Cobet in *Hermes* 105, 1977, 2–27; Fornara replies in *Hermes* 109, 1981, 149–56: the question remains a matter of argument.

On the opening, programmatic sentence of Herodotus' *History*, see the article by Hartmut Erbse (*Festschrift Bruno Snell*, Munich, 1956, 209–22), which provides a painstaking analysis of Herodotus' vocabulary and syntax: Erbse emphasizes the movement from the general to the particular and precise and the implied equivalence between Herodotus' 'enquiries' and the 'deeds' of the characters of his narrative. Tilman Krischer (*Hermes* 93, 1965, 159–67) carries the analysis further, emphasizing the echoes of the language of Greek epic.

The best and most helpful discussions of Herodotus' thinking and of his understanding of historical events are perhaps those by Henry R. Immerwahr, *Form and Thought in Herodotus* (Cleveland, 1966), H. F. Bornitz, *Herodot-Studien* (Berlin, 1968), Seth Bernadete, *Herodotean Inquiries* (The Hague,

1969), and C.W.Fornara, *Herodotus: an Interpretative essay* (Oxford, 1971): in different ways all four authors set out to analyze the conceptual unity of Herodotus' narrative. This unitary approach to Herodotus' text and thought goes back to earlier work by Otto Regenbogen ('Herodot und sein Werk', *Antike* 6 (1930), 202–48, reprinted along with much other important writing on Herodotus in W. Marg, ed., *Herodot* in the *Wege der Forschung* series, vol. 26, 2nd edn., Darmstadt, 1981 and by Friedrich Focke (*Herodot als Historiker*, Stuttgart, 1927). It represents a reaction from the 'analytical' assumptions of Jacoby and others (for example, Enoch Powell in his *History of Herodotus*, Cambridge, 1939). Attention has shifted decisively in recent work from a concern with the order of composition of Herodotus' narrative, based on the assumption that his own perception of his role developed from that of a traveller and ethnographer or collector of local traditions to that of 'historian', to an engagement with the nature and coherence of his text. There is a good and representative sample of the prevailing temper in Herodotean researches in *Herodotus and the Invention of History* (*Arethusa* 20, 1987).

On Herodotus' 'philosophy of history', the most balanced and well-argued account of the view against which I argue in Chapter 4 above seems to me to be the essay by D.M.Pippidi of 1960, reprinted in his *Parerga* (Bucharest and Paris, 1984), 28–42. In considering the historicity of Herodotus' narrative of the events of the Persian wars, especially of battles, we have to take account of the great difficulties we ourselves face in attempting to reconstruct 'what actually happened': there is a good, if somewhat dispiriting, discussion of such difficulties in a classic article by N.Whatley in *Journal of Hellenic Studies* 84 (1964), 119–39. Two detailed treatments of Herodotus' use of tradition about oracular responses (Roland Crahay, *La littérature oraculaire chez Hérodote*, Paris, 1956 and Jutta Kirchberg, *Die Funktion der Orakel im Werke Herodots*, Göttingen, 1965) offer very different approaches. Crahay is chiefly concerned with the historicity of Herodotus' reported oracles: he distinguishes 'religious' from 'political' responses and concludes that, while the former derive from oral tradition and represent genuine 'memory', the latter are almost entirely fictional and tendentious, the product of powerful interests, kings, tyrants and political leaders. His sceptical conclusions are taken further by Joseph Fontenrose, *The Delphic Oracle* (Berkeley, Los Angeles and London, 1978). Kirchberg's concern is with the meaning that traditions about oracles had for Herodotus: she accepts his belief in the veracity of the traditions and shows how oracular responses, which give access to divine knowledge, however dark and riddling, are a vital and indispensable part of Herodotus' perception of human history.

An interest in narrative has produced some stimulating recent work, in particular Mabel Lang's *Herodotean Narrative and Discourse* (Cambridge, Mass., 1984), Timothy Long's *Repetition and Variation in the Short Stories of Herodotus* (Frankfurt am Main, 1987) and Paavo Hohti's *The Interrelation of Speech and Action in the Histories of Herodotus* (Helsinki, 1976). The episode of Croesus and Solon in Book 1 is well analyzed in C.C. Chiasson's essay, 'The Herodotean Solon' (*Greek, Roman and Byzantine Studies* 27, 1986, 249–62). Chiasson considers the relationship between Solon's extant poetry (certainly known to Herodotus) and the *persona* created by Herodotus to serve the larger ends of his narrative. Three very different readings of the Croesus narrative are provided by Charles Segal in *Wiener Studien* n.s. 5 (1971), 39–51, by Hans-Peter Stahl in *Yale Classical Studies* 24 (1975), 1–36, and by T. A. Sebeok and E. Brady in *Quaderni Urbinati* n.s. 1 (1979), 7–22: their differing readings bring out well the complexities of Herodotus' text. For an historical analysis of the problems of Herodotus' account and in particular of its chronology, see J. A. S. Evans in *Classical Journal* 74, 1978, 34–40.

A pair of similarly complementary and illuminating readings of the episode of Gyges and Kandaules is offered by the essay of Hans-Peter Stahl in *Hermes* 96, 1968, 385–400 and the narratological and stylistic analysis produced by Timothy Long in *Repetition and Variation*, 9–38. J. A. S. Evans in *Greek, Roman and Byzantine Studies* 26 (1985), 229–33 suggests that Herodotus thought he was drawing on Lydian tradition for the story of Kandaules. In an important essay in *Hermes* 92 (1964), Erwin Wolff shows that the story of Gyges and Kandaules is closely echoed in the story of Xerxes and the wife of Masistes at the end of Herodotus' narrative in Book 9, an example of large-scale ring-form in the structuring of the *History*.

The most stimulating analyses of Herodotus' perception of space and of his attitude to the non-Greek world are Francois Hartog's brilliant book *Le miroir d'Hérodote* (Paris, 1980), on which see Chapter Five, note 6 above, and James Redfield's essay 'Herodotus the tourist' (*Classical Philology* 80 (1985), 97–118).

Herodotus' fluctuating reputation since the implicitly adverse judgment of Thucydides is plotted by J.A.S.Evans in *Classical Journal* 64 (1968), 11–17; in addition to the essays by Arnaldo Momigliano and Oswyn Murray cited in Chapter 6, notes 4 and 30 above, there is a good discussion of Herodotus' influence on the Hellenistic historian Hieronymus of Cardia in Jane Hornblower's *Hieronymus of Cardia* (Oxford, 1981), 137–53. On the place of women in Herodotus' accounts of non-Greek cultures, M.Rossellini and Suzanne Said offer a perceptive and persuasive reading in structuralist terms in their essay, 'Usages des femmes et autres *nomoi* chez les 'sauvages' d'Hérodote' (*Annali della Scuola Normale Superiore di Pisa*, ser. 3, 8 (1978), 949–1005). There are useful brief comments on the part played by women in Herodotus' narrative in Simon Hornblower's *Thucydides* (London, 1987), 14–16 and in Stewart Flory, *The Archaic Smile of Herodotus* (Detroit, 1987), 42–6.

Index

156

INDEX

Athens, 2, 12, 14–16, 42, 55, 70, 114, 116–18, 147
  acropolis of, 123
  National Museum, 34
  Sto Poikile, 35
Athos, 108
Atossa, 45, 130, 131
Atreus, 32, 64
Attaginos, 19
Attica, 13, 22
Atys, 53, 142
Azande, 71

Baal, priest of, 129
Babylon, 12, 66, 95, 109
  fall of (521 BC), 23, 113
Babylonians, 122
Bacchiad family, 131
Bacchylides, 35
Bactrian tribes, 66
Balkans, southern, 2
Barley, Nigel, 19, 26
Battiad kings of Cyrene, 40
Behistun, inscription at, 4, 48, 114
Benjamin, Walter, vii, 41, 81, 112
Berossus, 129
Bias, 21, 51, 124
Biton, 62
Bitter Lakes, 48
Black Sea, 12, 25
Bodrum, *see* Halicarnassus
Bogas, 35
Borysthenes river, 100
Bosphorus, 48, 107
Brauron, 46
Brindisi, 13
Buto, 75

Cadmus, 39
Caere, 13
calendars, 47
Callatiae, 95
Callimachus, 58
Cambyses, 1, 2, 24, 45, 51, 57, 65–6, 70, 74–5, 76, 94–5, 103–5, 106, 124
cannabis, 102
cannibalism, 32, 33, 105
Cape Taenarum, 30
Carians, 5–6, 30, 123
Carthaginians, 12
Castor, 46
Caunians, 123
causation, 63–85, 114–15, 120–1, 142
  parallel human and divine, 70–3

Ceians, 92
Celtic tribes, 12
Cheops, pyramid inscription, 24–5
Chios, 40
  inscription from, 28
Chorasmians, 106–7
chronicles, 47
chronology, 39–40, 45–6, 140
  lists of Hecataeus of Miletus, 40
  of stories of Croesus and Cyrus, 45
Chryses, 64
Cicilia, 88, 90
circumcision, 97
Cleobis, 62
Cleomenes, 81, 131
Cnidos, 108
Collingwood, R. G., 126
Colophon, 6, 8
Corcyra, 51–2
Corinth, 15, 49, 50, 55–7, 127
Corinthians, 51, 123
Crete, 51
Crimea, 13
Croesus, 21, 24, 39, 42, 44–5, 49, 51, 59, 61, 64, 65, 78, 100, 107, 116, 118, 121–2
  fall of, 1, 37–8, 53–4, 67–8, 79–80, 124
  krater gift, 31, 115
  traditions about, 34–5
  piety and generosity of, 125, 148
Ctesias, 67
Cyclopes, 76–7
Cydonia, 51
Cyprus, 12, 57
Cyrene, 12, 13, 40, 45, 46, 57, 73, 89
Cyrus the Great, 1, 2, 5, 24, 25, 37, 44–5, 59, 61, 65, 66, 68–9, 73, 78, 102–3, 105, 106, 107, 109, 116, 122, 123–5, 126–7
  stories of origins, 32–3
Cyzicus, 29

Danube, 85, 90, 107
Dareius, 1, 2, 4–5, 15, 22, 26, 27, 45, 46, 48, 57, 66–7, 70, 80, 83, 92, 95, 105, 107–8, 124
  inscriptions, 23, 127
David, 126
de Romilly, Jacqueline, 63, 115
de Ste Croix, Geoffrey, 72, 142, 150
Deioces, 45, 62
Delian league, 118
Delians, 91–2